THE FULL TUITION $CHOLARSHIP$ BOOK:

Pay Very Little For College

Chrisnuel Publishing

The Full Tuition Scholarships Book: Pay Very Little for College by Chrisnuel Publishing.

Published by Chrisnuel publishing.

Distributed by Amazon LLC.

Trademarks: Chrisnuel does not claim ownership of the on/around campus images used in the book as well as the organizational logos, registered trademarks or trade names of their respective holders.

They were all used with the sole purpose of profiling the institutions of which they describe. Furthermore, images were used following the fair use guidelines in regards to the scholarship and academic setting for which this book is exactly created for. The book was carefully crafted out for the good of the general public.

Credits: Quality research was done during the production of this book. We wish to acknowledge some highly helpful platforms from which accurate data was sourced – US news (*college data*), Educationdata.org (*student loan data*), and Wikipedia (*general inquiries*). Also credits to Pixabay for the illustration used on the book cover.

Disclaimer: The information listed in this book was curated to help students get a degree without having to owe thousands of dollars in student loan. The author and publisher have done proper research and put in their best efforts in this book. We are not in affiliation with any university/college listed in this book. Also, this book is not endorsed by any school or organization listed in it.

Although the best resources and research was put into the production of this book, it is sold with the understanding that neither the publisher nor the authors are engaged in rendering legal, accounting or other professional services. If legal advice or other expert assistance is required, the services of a competent professional person should be sought. Therefore, Chrisnuel specifically disclaim any responsibility for any liability, loss or risk, personal or otherwise, which is incurred as a consequence, directly or indirectly, of the use and application of any of the contents of this book.

This publication is designed to provide quality and authoritative information in regards to the subject matter covered here. However, the authors make no warranties in regards to the totality of the contents of the book and specifically disclaim any implied warranties or merchantability or fitness for a particular purpose. Therefore, the information, details, and opinions listed in here are not guaranteed to produce any particular results.

Printed and bound in the United States of America.

Table of Contents

<u>Dedication</u>

This book is dedicated to Almighty God and to all scholars – both U.S. and International – who wish to attend college on a full tuition scholarship and graduate with little to no debt.

May Your Wishes Come True !

A Sample View of Scholarships Listed.

Read Through To See "All The Scholarships" Listed in This Book →

(Listings are State by State — From Alabama down to Wyoming)

ALABAMA

Alabama State University

Location: Huntsville, Alabama
Setting: Urban (172 Acres)
Undergraduate Enrollment: 3,499
Type: Public

Academic Incentive Scholarship: Awards Full tuition and a $500 book award.

Requirements: A minimum ACT Score of 20 or a comparable SAT score of 1020 (EBR/W and math) | High school GPA of 3.0 or higher.

Black and Gold Scholarship: Awards Full tuition, required fees, and/or on campus room and board as follows:

The Black and Gold Scholarship pays $4,000 a year for a maximum of eight semesters for freshmen and a maximum of six semesters for college transfer students.

Requirements: A minimum ACT Score of 18 or a comparable SAT score of 940 (EBR/W and math) | High school GPA of 2.75 or higher.

Application Deadline: February 15

Application link:
https://www.alasu.edu/admissions/undergrad-admissions/asu-academic-scholarships

University of Alabama in Huntsville

Location: Huntsville, Alabama
Setting: City (432 Acres)
Undergraduate Enrollment: 7,569
Type: Public

Merit Tuition Scholarship: Awards Full tuition to incoming freshmen.

Requirements: A minimum ACT Score of 30 or SAT score of 1390 | High school GPA of 3.50.

National Merit Awards: Awards Full tuition, one year of on-campus housing at a regular room rate, course fees up to $500 per academic year and a one-time $3,000 UAH led summer study abroad allowance.

Eligibility: Applicant's must be recognized as National Merit Finalists.

Application Deadline: December 15

Application link:
https://www.uah.edu/admissions/undergraduate/financial-aid/scholarships/freshmen

The cost of attending college is expensive and the high cost of tuition is unarguably a major contributing factor to the high cost of acquiring a college degree.

The average cost of tuition at a 4-year institution is $19,020, or 53.5% of total college cost. This is more than half of the average cost of a college education. The statistics listed above is an average implying that there are a good number of colleges with a higher tuition rate.

Another alarming factor is that these tuition prices are steadily on the rise. Here is a typical example, the cost of tuition at public 4-year institutions increased by 31.4% from 2010 to 2020.

At this point, you may agree with me that exempting tuition and fees from the entire college cost sheet will make college cost to be a lot cheaper.

The overall cost of acquiring a college degree can range from $100,000 to $350,000 depending on the institution, major choice, residency, and a number of other factors. Exempting tuition will reduce the cost by more than half allowing people to pay far less and consequently making college more affordable.

Is this huge tuition waiver really possible?

The answer is YES. It is possible and open to everyone.

Now, you may want to ask HOW?

It is possible through Full Tuition Scholarships. These scholarships typically cover tuition and fees for students.

Take a brief look at another statistics.

In the consumer debt category, student loan debt is ranked No. 2 only surpassed by mortgages. Student loan debt in the United States totals **$1.748 trillion.** The outstanding federal loan balance is **$1.620 trillion** and accounts for 92.7% of all student loan debt.

High tuition cost is a major contributor in this student loan numbers.

Data Source -- educationdata.org/average-cost-of-college
Data Source -- educationdata.org/college-tuition-inflation-rate

Further alarming statistics:

- The average student borrower takes 20 years to pay off their student loan debt.
- Some professional graduates take over 45 years to repay student loans.
- 21% of borrowers see their total student loan debt balance increase in the first 5 years of their loan.

Taking a student loan seems to be the easy way out. This is because scholars who take student loan(s) will not have to worry about the financing of their college education until graduation, but the seeming reality is that loan takers may have to spend a decade or more after graduation playing catch-up in their finances.

Finally, you should agree that having a scholarship award that covers the full tuition for all four years will go a long way in cutting down college costs enabling students to pay very little for a college education.

This book is equipped with privileged information on Full Tuition Scholarships that are awarded by various institutions across the United States. These scholarships will enable scholars to attend college at a very little cost by offsetting the huge cost of tuition.

———— *Data Source -- educationdata.org/average-time-to-repay-student-loans*

Scholarships Renewal

Scholars who are privileged to receive a full tuition scholarship must however note that certain renewal requirements need to be met to retain the scholarship award. The journey does not just end in the initial earning of the award, the scholar(s) has to keep on exuding the excellence that earned them the scholarship at first.

The renewal requirements for the respective full tuition scholarships vary, therefore the scholar should ensure that the renewal requirement(s) for the full tuition award they have received are duly met.

We wish you every success in getting a full tuition scholarship and making the most of it.

✍ **Note: For Paperback readers, pages will appear in black & white. For eBook readers, pages will appear in color.**

Some links may change due to constantly evolving Colleges' website. Check for the scholarship(s) on the school's website.

CHAPTER 1

FULL TUITION INSTITUTIONAL SCHOLARSHIPS

1 University of Alabama

Location: Tuscaloosa, Alabama
Setting: Suburban (1,143 Acres)
Undergraduate Enrollment: 31,685
Type: Public

Presidential Scholarship: Awards Full tuition scholarship to **in-state students**.

Requirements: A minimum ACT Score of 30 or SAT score of 1360 | High school GPA of 3.50+

Application Deadline: October 31 (Application deadline for the first round)

Application link:
https://scholarships.ua.edu/freshman/in-state/

2 Alabama State University

Location: Huntsville, Alabama
Setting: Urban (172 Acres)
Undergraduate Enrollment: 3,499
Type: Public

Academic Incentive Scholarship: Awards Full tuition and a $500 book award.

Requirements: A minimum ACT Score of 20 or a comparable SAT score of 1020 (EBR/W and math) | High school GPA of 3.0 or higher.

Black and Gold Scholarship: Awards Full tuition, required fees, and/or on campus room and board as follows:

The Black and Gold Scholarship pays $4,000 a year for a maximum of eight semesters for freshmen and a maximum of six semesters for college transfer students.

Requirements: A minimum ACT Score of 18 or a comparable SAT score of 940 (EBR/W and math) | High school GPA of 2.75 or higher.

Application Deadline: February 15

Application link:
https://www.alasu.edu/admissions/undergrad-admissions/asu-academic-scholarships

3 University of Alabama in Huntsville

Location: Huntsville, Alabama
Setting: City (432 Acres)
Undergraduate Enrollment: 7,569
 Type: Public

Merit Tuition Scholarship: Awards Full tuition to incoming freshmen.

Requirements: A minimum ACT Score of 30 or SAT score of 1390 | High school GPA of 3.50.

National Merit Awards: Awards Full tuition, one year of on-campus housing at a regular room rate, course fees up to $500 per academic year and a one-time $3,000 UAH led summer study abroad allowance.

Eligibility: Applicant's must be recognized as National Merit Finalists.

Application Deadline: December 15

Application link:
https://www.uah.edu/admissions/undergraduate/financial-aid/scholarships/freshmen

4 University of South Alabama

Location: Mobile, Alabama
Setting: Suburban (1,224 Acres)
Undergraduate Enrollment: 8,833
 Type: Public

USA Freshman Admission Scholarship: Awards Full tuition.

Eligibility: Applicant must be a U.S. citizen, applied for/obtained Permanent residency, or a student attending a U.S. High school with a qualified visa status.

Requirements: A minimum ACT Score of 32 or SAT score of 1420 | High school GPA of 3.50.

Application Deadline: December 1

Application link:
https://www.southalabama.edu/departments/financialaffairs/scholarships/freshscholarships/

5 University of Alabama at Birmingham

Location: Birmingham, Alabama
Setting: Urban (437 Acres)
Undergraduate Enrollment: 13,547
Type: Public

Presidential Recognition: Awards Full tuition and fees to **in-state students**.

Requirements: A minimum ACT Score of 30 or SAT equivalent | High school GPA of 3.50 or higher.

Presidential Scholarship for National Scholars: Awards Full tuition and fees, one year on campus housing allotment, one time $2,500 experiential learning stipend and one-year $1,000 Provost First year Scholarship.

Eligibility: National Merit Finalists and National Hispanic Recognition Program Scholars.

Application Deadline: April 1 for the June intake. May 1 for the August intake. November 1 for the January intake.

Application link:
https://www.uab.edu/admissions/cost/scholarships/in-state-students

6 Alabama A&M University

Location: Montgomery, Alabama
Setting: Urban (1,173 Acres)
Undergraduate Enrollment: 5,107
Type: Public

The AAMU Merit Scholarship: Award covers the cost of tuition.

Requirements: A minimum ACT Score of 23 or SAT score of 1130 | High school GPA of 3.25+

There are other additional Scholarships.

Application Deadline: February 28

Application link:
https://www.aamu.edu/admissions-aid/financial-aid/scholarships/index.html

1 University of the Ozarks

Location: Clarksville, Arkansas
Setting: Rural (45 Acres)
Undergraduate Enrollment: 784
Type: Private

Full Need Tuition Scholarship:
Awards need-based full tuition scholarship to Arkansas students from Johnson, Logan, Franklin, Madison, and Newton counties.

Check here for more information:
https://ozarks.edu/news/full-need-tuition-scholarship/

Requirements: Top Applicants.

Application Deadline: Check site for application procedure.

Application link:
https://ozarks.edu/admissions-aid/costs-and-aid/grants-and-scholarships/

2 John Brown University

Location: Siloam Springs, Arkansas
Setting: City (200 Acres)
Undergraduate Enrollment: 1,617
Type: Private

Presidential Scholarship: Awards $27,500. This covers the total cost of tuition.

Requirements: A minimum 3.6 cumulative high school GPA | ACT score of 32+ or SAT score of 1420+ (Applicant's can make up for a low GPA with high test scores and vice versa)

Application Deadline: November 5 (Fall) | March 4 (Spring)

Application link: https://www.jbu.edu/financial-aid/on-campus-undergraduate/scholarships-and-aid/scholarships/

3 Hendrix College

Location: Conway, Arkansas
Setting: Subruban (175 Acres)
Undergraduate Enrollment: 1,111
Type: Private

Provost Scholarship: Awards Full tuition.

Requirements: ACT Score of 32 or SAT score of 1430 | High school GPA of 3.6

President's & Madison Murphy Leadership Scholarship: Full tuition, board, half the room.

Requirements: ACT Score of 32 or SAT score of 1430 | High school GPA of 3.6

Application Deadline: November 15

Application link: https://www.hendrix.edu/financialaid/scholarships/

4 Harding University

Location: Searcy, Arkansas
Setting: Subruban (350 Acres)
Undergraduate Enrollment: 3,687
Type: Private

Trustee Scholar Award: Award covers Full tuition.

Requirements: 31+ ACT composite score, 1390+ SAT combined critical reading and math score | A minimum 3.5 high school GPA.

There are other available Scholarships.

Application Deadline: March 15

Application link; https://www.harding.edu/admissions/scholarships

5 Lyon College

Location: Batesville, Arkansas
Setting: City (136 Acres)
Undergraduate Enrollment: 580
Type: Private

Honors Fellows Program: A Fellow receives an annual stipend up to the cost of tuition.

Trustee Scholarship: Awards up to Full tuition.

Requirements: Top Applicants.

Application Deadline: Check site for more details.

Application link: https://www.lyon.edu/scholarships-aid-programs

6 Philander Smith College

Location: Little Rock, Arkansas
Setting: Urban (9 Acres)
Undergraduate Enrollment: 710
Type: Private

Thomas Mason Scholarship: Full tuition and Fees.

Requirements: A minimum 3.2 high school GPA | ACT composite score of 21 | SAT composite score of 1060.

Application Deadline: Check site for more details.

Application link: https://www.philander.edu/admissions/paying-for-college/scholarships

7 Williams Baptist College

Location: Walnut Ridge, Arkansas
Setting: Rural (250 Acres)
Undergraduate Enrollment: 577
Type: Private

President's Scholarship: Awards $10,000 per year. (This covers the total cost of tuition)

Requirements: ACT 22-26 / SAT equivalent.

Founders Scholarship: Awards $12,000 per year. (This covers the total cost of tuition)

Requirements: ACT 27+ / SAT equivalent.

Application Deadline: June 1

Application link: https://williamsbu.edu/financial-aid/scholarships/

8 Ouachita Baptist University

Location: Arkadelphia, Arkansas
Setting: Rural (200 Acres)
Undergraduate Enrollment: 1,716
Type: Private

President's Scholarship: Awards $18,500/year (This covers the total cost of tuition)

Requirements: High school GPA of 4.0 or higher.

Founder's Scholarship: Awards $15,000/year (This covers the total cost of tuition)

Requirements: High school GPA of 3.85-3.99.

Application Deadline: January 15

Application link: https://obu.edu/finaid/obu.php

1 University of Arizona

Location: Tucson, Arizona
Setting: City (392 Acres)
Undergraduate Enrollment: 38,528
Type: Public

All-Arizona Academic Team Award: Awards full tuition scholarship to *Arizona residents*.

Eligibility: Applicant must be a U.S. citizen or permanent resident or demonstrate lawful immigration status | Top applicants.

Arizona Academy Scholars Tuition Award: Provides $8,000 - $12,500 per academic year.

(This covers the total cost of tuition)

The Arizona Academy is UArizona's premier opportunity for international high school students to earn university credit while still enrolled in secondary school.

Requirements: Students must successfully complete the Arizona Academy program | Top applicants.

2 Northern Arizona University

Location: Flagstaff, Arizona
Setting: City (829 Acres)
Undergraduate Enrollment: 24,168
Type: Public

Lumberjack Scholars Award: Awards full tuition scholarship to *Arizona residents*.

Requirements: A minimum 3.5 unweighted core high school GPA | Top applicants.

Application Deadline: August 1 (Fall) | December 1 (Spring)

Application link: https://nau.edu/office-of-scholarships-and-financial-aid/freshman-merit-based-tuition-scholarships/

Arizona Tuition Award: Awards $1,000 - $35,000 per academic year. (This covers the total cost of tuition)

Eligibility: Applicant must be a U.S. citizen or permanent resident or demonstrate lawful immigration status | Be classified as a *non-Arizona* resident | Top applicants.

Application Deadline: May 3

Application link: https://financialaid.arizona.edu/types-of-aid/scholarships/2021-2022-terms-and-conditions

1 University of California - Davis

Location: Davis, California
Setting: City (5,300 Acres)
Undergraduate Enrollment: 31,657
Type: Public

UC Davis' Scholarships: The scholarships can range from $100 to $14,000 per academic year. (This covers the base tuition for california residents)

UC Blue and Gold Opportunity Plan: The Blue and Gold Opportunity Plan ensures that eligible California undergraduates with an annual family income of less than $80,000 will have their systemwide – or base – tuition and fees covered by gift aid.

Requirements: A minimum 3.25 GPA.

Application Deadline: November 30

Application link:
https://financialaid.ucdavis.edu/scholarships/campus

2 California Lutheran University

Location: Thousand Oaks, California
Setting: Suburban (290 Acres)
Undergraduate Enrollment: 2,592
Type: Private

Presidential Scholarship: Awards $25,000 up to Full tuition.

Requirements: This scholarship is awarded to graduating high school seniors in the top tier of the application pool.

Steven Dorfman Scholarship: 75% up to full tuition.

Requirements: Top Applicants.

Application Deadline: November 15

Application link:
https://www.callutheran.edu/financial-aid/scholarships-grants/undergraduate.html

3 Saint Mary's College of California

Location: Moraga, Carlifornia
Setting: Suburban (420 Acres)
Undergraduate Enrollment: 2,199
Type: Private

The East Bay Performing Arts Scholarship for Black Students or Students of African Descent: Awards Full tuition.

Requirements: The recipient must agree to major or minor in the program awarding the scholarship.

Mentored Access to Programs in Science (MAPS): Awards Full tuition.

Eligibility: This scholarship is awarded to high achieving students with financial need interested in studying Biology, Mathematics, Physics, Chemistry, or Biochemistry.

Check here for more details: https://www.stmarys-ca.edu/school-of-science/mentored-access-to-programs-in-science-maps

Application Deadline: January 15

Application link: https://www.stmarys-ca.edu/undergraduate-admissions/first-year-freshmen-scholarships

4 University of Southern California

Location: Los Angeles, Carlifornia
Setting: Urban (226 Acres)
Undergraduate Enrollment: 20,790
Type: Private

Mork Family Scholarship: Awards Full tuition plus $5000/year additional housing stipend.

Trustee Scholarship: Awards Full tuition.

Requirements: Application is open to incoming freshmen through the USC Office of Admission. Candidates are selected from an extremely competitive pool.

Application Deadline: December 1

Application link: https://financialaid.usc.edu/undergraduates/admitted/scholarships.html

5 Loyola Marymount University

Location: Los Angeles, California
Setting: Suburban (142 Acres)
Undergraduate Enrollment: 7,127
Type: Private

Arrupe Scholarships: Awards up to full tuition for all four (4) years.

Requirements: Recipients are selected from among the best applicants.

Application Deadline: Contact Admission Office.

Application link:
https://financialaid.lmu.edu/prospectivestudents/scholarships/lmuacademicscholarshipsforfirst-yearstudents/

6 Harvey Mudd College

Location: Claremont, Carlifornia
Setting: Suburban (33 Acres)
Undergraduate Enrollment: 905
Type: Private

President's Scholars Program: Full tuition scholarship which is renewable for four (4) years.

Requirements: Applicant(s) must be a U.S. citizen or permanent resident | Have a proven record of academic success with excellent grades | Show leadership capabilities.

Application Deadline: January 20

Application link:
https://www.hmc.edu/admission/afford/scholarships-and-grants/merit-based-scholarships/presidents-scholars-program/

7

Claremont McKenna College

Location: Claremont, Carlifornia
Setting: Suburban (69 Acres)
Undergraduate Enrollment: 1,416
Type: Private

Seaver Scholars Program: Scholarship awards full tuition for all four (4) years.

Requirements: Students who demonstarte exceptional leadership promise along with a commitment to making a positive impact in the world.

Application Deadline: Contact Admission Office.

Application link: https://www.cmc.edu/admission/scholarships

Interdisciplinary Science Scholars: Scholarship awards full Science tuition scholars for all four (4) years + plus summer fellowships, internships, or research experiences.

Requirements: Students with a passion for Science and Leadership.

Application Deadline: Contact Admission Office.

Application link: https://www.cmc.edu/admission/scholarships

1 Colorado Christian University

Location: Lakewood, Colorado
Setting: Suburban (53 Acres)
Undergraduate Enrollment: 7,188
Type: Private

World Changers Scholarship: Awards Full tuition.

Requirements: A minimum ACT score of 28 or SAT composite score of 1320 | 3.8 high school GPA.

P.S: The World Changers Scholarship competition is by invitation only.

Application Deadline: December 20

Application link:
https://www.ccu.edu/undergrad/financial-aid/scholarships/ccu-scholarships/

2 Colorado Mesa University

Location: Grand Junction, Colorado
Setting: City (86 Acres)
Undergraduate Enrollment: 8,712
Type: Public

Distinguished Scholar (*Colorado Resident*): Awards Full tuition.

Requirements: A minimum 3.75 high school GPA (weighted) | ACT composite score of 29 | SAT combined score of 1340 | Top 5% of their Class.

CMU and Donor Scholarships: These scholarships range from a cash stipend to full tuition and fees.

Housing Scholarships are available for prospective students.

Application Deadline: December 31

Application link:
https://www.coloradomesa.edu/financial-aid/scholarships/freshmen.html

3 University of Colorado, Colorado Springs

Location: Colorado Springs, Colorado
Setting: Urban (550 Acres)
Undergraduate Enrollment: 10,002
Type: Public

UCCS Chancellor's Award: This $10,000 scholarship covers the total cost of Tuition, Books and Supplies and other Fees for **in-state students**.

Peak Scholarship: This $25,000 scholarship covers the total cost of Tuition, Books and Supplies and other Fees for **out-of-state students**.

Requirements: Top Applicants.

Application Deadline: Admitted students can apply between Dec 1 – May 1 for the upcoming aid year.

Application link: https://www.uccs.edu/degreesandprograms/scholarships-uccs

4 Colorado College

Location: Colorado Springs, Colorado
Setting: City (100 Acres)
Undergraduate Enrollment: 2,241
Type: Private

Barnes Scholars

Otis A. and Margaret T. Barnes: Awards Full tuition.

Otis A. and Margaret T. Barnes established two trusts that provide full tuition scholarships to Colorado College. The first is to be used for awards in Chemistry and Biochemistry, and the second for awards in Biology, Environmental Sciences, Geology, Mathematics, Physics, and Psychology (including Neuroscience).

Requirements: Top Applicants.

Application Deadline: November 1

Application link: https://www.coloradocollege.edu/admission/financialaid/scholarships/index.html

5

Regis University

Location: Denver, Colorado
Setting: Suburban (90 Acres)
Undergraduate Enrollment: 2,745
Type: Private

Presidential Catholic Schools Scholarship: Awards Full tuition scholarship to residential students.

Eligibility: High achieving graduating seniors from parochial high schools within the United States and Puerto Rico are eligible for this scholarship.

Requirements: Graduating seniors must be nominated by their high school principals or secondary school counselors.

Connors Scholarship: Awards Full tuition.

Eligibility: Applicant must have an affiliation with a Boston area services organization | Have a cumulative recalculated high school GPA of at least 3.5

Massachusetts Nursing Association COVID-19 Scholarship: Awards Full tuition.

Eligibility: Applicant must be the dependent of a member of the Massachusetts Nursing Associate who has been working on the front lines during the COVID-19 pandemic | Plan to major in nursing or a health related field | A recalculated high school GPA of at least 3.5

Regis College Puerto Dear Neighbor Scholarship: Awards Full tuition scholarship to residential students who demonstrate the values of the Sisters of Saint Joseph of Boston.

These values include:

✓ Gracious hospitality

✓ Love and service of the Dear Neighbor without distinction

✓ Peaceful resolution of conflict

✓ Care for all God's creation.

Sloane Scholarship: Awards Full tuition.

Requirements: Applicant must plan to major in a program within the Sloane School of Business and Communication | A recalculated high school GPA of at least 3.5

Application Deadline: January 1

Application link:
https://www.regiscollege.edu/admission-and-aid/undergraduate-admission/cost-and-financial-aid/scholarships

1 University of Connecticut

Location: Storrs, Connecticut
Setting: Rural (4,076 Acres)
Undergraduate Enrollment: 18,567
Type: Public

Presidential Scholars Award: Covers the Full cost of tuition plus a one-time $2,500 enrichment award. *(Available only to Connecticut students)*

Requirements: Applicant must be a Valedictorian/Salutatorian to be considered for this award | A Connecticut resident graduating from a Connecticut high school.

Leadership Scholarship: Awards Full tuition to **in-state students** and half tuition for **out-of-state students.**

Requirements: Top Applicants.

Application Deadline: December 1

Application link: https://admissions.uconn.edu/cost-aid/scholarship/

2 Western Connecticut State University

Location: Danbury, Connecticut
Setting: Urban (398 Acres)
Undergraduate Enrollment: 4,641
Type: Public

President-to-President Scholarship: In-state tuition and fees for 2 years.

Requirements: Awarded to an outstanding graduating Naugatuck Valley Community College student who has been accepted to WSCU | A minimum 3.3 GPA.

Application Deadline: March 1

Application link: https://www.wcsu.edu/admissions/merit-scholarships/

University of Delaware

Location: Newark, Delaware
Setting: Suburban (1,996 Acres)
Undergraduate Enrollment: 18,671
Type: Private-Public

ROTC Scholarships

U.S. Air Force ROTC: There are three different types of scholarships under this category.

Please refer to this site for more details…

https://www.afrotc.com/scholarships/

This award covers full tuition and authorized fees, plus a monthly living expense stipend and an annual book stipend.

Requirements: U.S. citizens | SAT composite score of 1240 or ACT composite score of 26 | A minimum cumulative unweighted GPA of 3.0 | Applicant must be physically fit.

Application Deadline: January 14

Application link: https://www.udel.edu/students/student-financial-services/undergraduate/

1 Florida Institute of Technology

Location: Melbourne, Florida
Setting: Suburban (174 Acres)
Undergraduate Enrollment: 3,496
Type: Private

Panther Distinguished Scholar Award *(Available only to Florida Residents)*: This is a combination of scholarships and grants that covers full tuition plus the facilities and activities fees to attend Florida Tech.

Eligibility: High school students who qualify for the Bright Futures Florida Academic Scholars (FAS) award are eligible to be considered for this scholarship.

Application Deadline: February 1

Application link: https://www.fit.edu/admissions/scholarships--aid/

2 Full Sail University

Location: Winter Park, Florida
Setting: Urban (200 Acres)
Undergraduate Enrollment: 19,171
Type: Private

Emerging Technology Scholarship: This is a full scholarship that covers full tuition and provides a laptop.

Eligibility: A cummulative high school GPA of 3.8 or higher, 1133 in SAT or higher (25 ACT or higher) | Meet admissions requirements for an eligible Bachelor of Science degree

Application Deadline: June 26

Application link: https://www.fullsail.edu/scholarships/emerging-technology-scholarship

Women in Technology Scholarship: This is a full scholarship that covers full tuition and provides a laptop.

Eligibility: Identify as a female | A cummulative high school GPA of 3.8 or higher, 1133 in SAT or higher (25 ACT or higher) | Meet admissions requirements for an eligible Bachelor of Science degree

Application Deadline: June 26

Application link: https://www.fullsail.edu/scholarships/women-in-technology-scholarship

3 Florida International University

Location: Miami, Florida
Setting: Urban (344 Acres)
Undergraduate Enrollment: 46,079
Type: Public

FIU College Board Recognition Program Scholarship: Awards Full tuition and fees, a book stipend plus a $1,000 meal plan stipend per semester.

Requirements: Applicant must be a U.S citizen, a U.S. lawful permanent resident or an international student with intention of receiving the F-1 visa to study in the United States | Awarded one of the recognition awards below from the College Board:

✓ African American Recognition
✓ Hispanic Recognition
✓ Indigenous Recognition
✓ Rural and Small Town Recognition

Presidential Merit Scholarship: Awards Full tuition and fees, plus a book stipend.

4 Stetson University

Location: DeLand, Florida
Setting: Suburban (185 Acres)
Undergraduate Enrollment: 2,884
Type: Private

Global Citizen Scholarship: Awards Full tuition scholarship to students who display characteristics of a global citizen.

Requirements: A minimum GPA of 3.5 | Applicant must submit a 500 word or less Essay to admissions@stetson.edu - How will your education prepare you to be a global citizen?

Students eligible to apply must be from one of the following reions:

❖ Americas – Andes, Southern Cone
❖ Middle East, North Africa and Central Asia
❖ Sub-Saharan Africa – East and Southern.

Application Deadline: March 1

Application link: https://www.stetson.edu/administration/financial-aid/scholarships/

Requirements: 4.0 GPA | A minimum SAT score of 1370 or ACT score of 30 or Top 5% of a Florida High School Graduating Class | Applicant must be a U.S citizen, a U.S. lawful permanent resident or an international student with intention of receiving the F-1 visa to study in the United States.

Application Deadline: January 31

Application link: https://scholarships.fiu.edu/browse-scholarships/merit-scholarships/index.html

1 LaGrange College

Location: LaGrange, Georgia
Setting: Rural (120 Acres)
Undergraduate Enrollment: 583
Type: Private

The Presidential Learning Scholarship: Awards Full tuition.

Requirements: Top applicants.

Application Deadline: January 1

Application link:
https://www.lagrange.edu/admission-and-aid/financial-aid/types-of-aid/Scholarships.html

2 Emory University

Location: Atlanta, Georgia
Setting: City (631 Acres)
Undergraduate Enrollment: 7,130
Type: Private

Courtesy Tuition Benefit: Awards Full tuition Scholarship to dependent children of eligible Emory Faculty and Staff based on employee hire date and years of service.

Requirements: Top applicants.

Application Deadline: November 15

Application link:
https://studentaid.emory.edu/undergraduate/types/emory-college/grants-scholarships/institution.html

3 Brenau University

Location: Gainesville, Georgia
Setting: City (57 Acres)
Undergraduate Enrollment: 1,427
Type: Private

Women's College Academic Scholarships

The Brenau Scholars Program: Awards Full tuition scholarship to residential students.

Requirements: A minimum ACT Score of 27 or SAT score of 1270 | High school GPA of 3.50+

Application Deadline: February 1

Application link:
https://www.brenau.edu/admissions/womenscollege/womens-college-academic-scholarships/

4 University of Georgia

Location: Athens, Georgia
Setting: City (767 Acres)
Undergraduate Enrollment: 30,166
Type: Public

There are no available full tuition scholarships at the University of Georgia. However, there are other scholarships that could be highly beneficial to incoming freshmen.

Please refer to this site for more details:
https://www.admissions.uga.edu/afford/scholarships/

5 Georgia Southern University

Location: Statesboro, Georgia
Setting: Rural (900 Acres)
Undergraduate Enrollment: 23,542
Type: Public

HOPE/Zell Miller Scholarship (*Available only to Georgia Residents*): Awards Full tuition.

Requirements: A minimum High school GPA of 3.7 | A minimum ACT composite score of 26 or a comparable SAT score of 1,200 (Reading and Math)

Application Deadline: February 1

Application link:
https://em.georgiasouthern.edu/finaid/hope-scholarship/

6 Savannah State University

Location: Savannah, Georgia
Setting: City (201 Acres)
Undergraduate Enrollment: 3,148
Type: Public

Zell Miller Scholarship (*Available only to Georgia Residents*): Awards Full tuition.

Requirements: Applicant must be a Valedictorian or Salutatorian for their graduating class; or received a score of at least 1,200 combined critical reading score and math score on a single administration of the SAT or an ACT composite scale score of at least 26 | A minimum High school GPA of 3.7

Application Deadline: Check site for more details.

Application link:
https://www.savannahstate.edu/financial-aid/types-of-aid/ssu-scholarships.shtml

Mercer University

7

Location: Macon, Georgia
Setting: City (150 Acres)
Undergraduate Enrollment: 4,941
Type: Private

Mercer Presidential Scholarship: Award Varies: Pays tuition, university fees, room, and board not covered by another scholarship.

Requirements: A minimum ACT Score of 28 | Applicant must be receiving the Western Centennial Scholarship.

Business Scholarship Challenge: The award may range up to Full tuition.

Learn more: https://undergrad.mercer.edu/visit-campus/

Requirements: Applicant must be interested in pursuing a major in Mercer's Stetson-Hatcher School of Business | Top Applicants.

Zell Miller Scholarship (Available only to Georgia Residents): Awards Full tuition.

Requirements: Applicant must be a Valedictorian or Salutatorian for their graduating class with a minimum GPA of 3.7 | A minimum ACT Score of 26 or SAT score of 1200.

P.S: ROTC Room and Board Scholarships are also available.

Application Deadline: November 15 (Early -Action) | February 1 (Priority Scholarship)

Application link: https://undergrad.mercer.edu/financial-planning/

8

Wesleyan College

Location: Macon, Georgia
Setting: Suburban (200 Acres)
Undergraduate Enrollment: 695
Type: Private

Lane Scholars Program: Awards Full tuition.

Requirements: Applicant must intend to major in the area of Fine Arts | A minimum High school GPA of 3.0 | Top Applicants.

Findlay Scholars Program: Awards Full tuition.

Requirements: Applicant must intend to major in either the Humanities or Social Sciences | A minimum High school GPA of 3.49 | Top Applicants.

Munroe Scholars Program: Awards Full tuition plus a research stipend of up to $1,000.

Requirements: Applicant must intend to major in the Sciences, Mathematics, or dual-degree Engineering | A minimum High school GPA of 3.5 | Top Applicants.

Mary Knox Mcneill Scholars Program: Awards Full tuition scholarship to students who demonstrate a commitment to faith and community service.

Requirements: A minimum High school GPA of 3.25 | Check site for more details.

Margaret Pitts Scholarship: Awards Full tuition scholarship to students who are active members of the United Methodist Church.

Requirements: A minimum High school GPA of 3.0 | Top Applicants.

Application Deadline: February 15

Application link: https://www.wesleyancollege.edu/admission/invitation-scholarships.cfm

9

Georgia Institute of Technology

Location: Atlanta, Georgia
Setting: Urban (400 Acres)
Undergraduate Enrollment: 17,447
Type: Public

Neilsen Foundation Scholarship: This scholarship provides Full tuition for in-state students and 125% of in-state tuition cost for out-of-state students.

Eligibility: Applicant must be in good academic standing | Undergraduate or Graduate students (enrolled online or on campus) who have experienced **neurological and functional impairment** due to a traumatic **spinal cord injury**, a **degenerative disease primary to the spinal cord**, or **damage to the spinal cord due to tumors or surgery.**

CyberCorps Scholarship for Service: Awards Full tuition and stipend to students in exchange for commitments to serve the U.S. Government in a cybersecurity role after graduation.

Requirements: Applicantion is open to students who are enrolled in the Computer Science, the Electrical and Computer Engineering, the Public Policy or International Affairs departments at Georgia Tech | Applicant must demonstrate strong interest in the field of cybersecurity.

Application Deadline: March 24

Application link: https://finaid.gatech.edu/undergraduate-types-aid/scholarships/

10

Oglethorpe University

Location: Atlanta, Georgia
Setting: Suburban (100 Acres)
Undergraduate Enrollment: 1,446
Type: Private

James Edward Oglethorpe: Awards Full tuition + Stipend for a junior year study abroad experience.

Civic Engagement: Awards Full tuition and an internship with a non-profit organization.

Oglethorpe Theatre: Awards Full tuition and an internship with a professional theatre company.

Hammack Business: Awards Full tuition + Stipend for study abroad or internship experience.

P.S: Full tuition awards are determined by performance at Oglethorpe's Scholarship Weekend. Scholarship Weekend is by invitation only.

Check site for more details: https://oglethorpe.edu/scholarshipweekend/

Application Deadline: November 1

Application link: https://oglethorpe.edu/admission/undergraduate-admission/scholarships-and-aid/

11 Spelman College

Location: Atlanta, Georgia
Setting: Urban (39 Acres)
Undergraduate Enrollment: 2,417
Type: Private

Dewitt Dean's Scholarship: Award covers full tuition for four years.

Requirements: A minimum SAT score of 1330 or 31 ACT | A minimum High school GPA of 3.8 (weighted)

Application Deadline: February 1

Application link: https://www.spelman.edu/admissions/financial-aid/scholarships

12 Piedmont College

Location: Demorest, Georgia
Setting: Rural (370 Acres)
Undergraduate Enrollment: 1,255
Type: Private

Piedmont Premier Scholarship: This scholarship may provide **up to the cost of tuition** and will be reduced by any state and institutional aid a student receives.

Requirements: Applicant must be a Valedictorian of a HOPE eligible high school from the state of Georgia.

Application Deadline: February 15

Application link: https://piedmont.smartcatalogiq.com/en/2020-2021/undergraduate-catalog/financial-aid/scholastic-achievement-awards/institutional-scholarship-programs/

1

University of Hawaii

Location: Honolulu, Hawaii

Setting: Urban (320 Acres)

Undergraduate Enrollment: 14,120

Type: Public

The Reagents and Presidential Scholarships covers the cost of tuition, and includes a $4000 stipend per year.

Eligibility: Reagents Scholarships are awarded to outstanding freshmen who has a minimum SAT total score of at least 1340 or ACT combined score of at least 29 | A minimum High school GPA of 3.5

Application Deadline: January 15

Application link: https://www.hawaii.edu/offices/student-affairs/regents-and-presidential-scholars-program/

1

University of Idaho

Location: Moscow, Idaho
Setting: Rural (810 Acres)
Undergraduate Enrollment: 8,366
Type: Public

National Merit Scholarship: This award covers basic registration fees/tuition and the university defined cost for room and board as long as you live in a U of I residence hall.

Requirements: Achieve Finalist standing with the National Merit Scholarship Corporation.

Application Deadline: May 31

Application link: https://www.uidaho.edu/financial-aid/scholarships/undergraduate/hs-resident

ROTC Military Scholarships

United States Army ROTC: This program offers 3.5 year, 3 year, 2.5 year and 2 year on campus scholarships that will pay for in/out state tuition and fees, pay $510 for books annually, and give at least $250 per month as a stipend while in school.

Call: University of Idaho Army ROTC for application at 208-885-6528

United States Air Force ROTC: This program offers scholarships to students who have at least two years remaining towards their bachelor degree when the scholarship starts. Awards full tuition, books, fees, and a monthly stipend during the academic year.

Call: University of Idaho Unit Admissions Officer, AFROTC Detachment 905, at 208-885-6129 or 800-622-5088.

United States Navy/Marine ROTC: This program offers scholarships to students selected through national competition. It covers college tuition, lab fees, books, uniforms, and includes a monthly stipend.

Call: University of Idaho, Commanding Officer, Naval Science Department at 208-885-6333.

Please refer to this site for more details: https://www.uidaho.edu/financial-aid/scholarships/undergraduate/hs-non-resident

1 University of Illinois

Location: Urbana-Champaign, Illinois
Setting: City (1,783 Acres)
Undergraduate Enrollment: 34,779
Type: Public

James Hunter Anthony & Gerald E. Blackshear Endowment: Awards up to full tuition and fees for an academic year.

Requirements: Illinois Resident who have graduated from an Illinois high school | Top applicants.

Provost Scholarship: Awards full tuition.

Requirements: Top Applicants.

Application Deadline: December 1

Application link: https://www.admissions.illinois.edu/invest/scholarships-all

2 Lewis University

Location: Romeoville, Illinois
Setting: Suburban (410 Acres)
Undergraduate Enrollment: 3,907
Type: Private

St. John Baptist DeLaSalle Scholarship: Awards full tuition.

Requirements: Top Applicants.

Application Deadline: January 15

Application link: https://www.lewisu.edu/admissions/finaid/scholarships.htm

3 University of Illinois at Chicago

Location: Chicago, Illinois
Setting: Urban (240 Acres)
Undergraduate Enrollment: 22,279
Type: Public

Lake County, Indiana Tuition Award: The value of this award varies. It can cover up to full in-sate tuition.

P.S: This four-year award program, administered to new incoming first-year and transfer students who are residents of Lake County, Indiana gives recipients the opportunity to study at UIC for the equivalent of in-state tuition.

Requirements: Applicant must be graduating from a high school in Lake County, Indiana | Top applicants.

Tribal Nation Tuition Award: The value of this award varies. It can cover up to full in-sate tuition.

P.S: This four-year grant program, administered to new incoming first-year and transfer students who are members of any of the 573 tribal nations recognized by the Bureau of Indian Affairs, gives recipients the opportunity to study at UIC for the equivalent of in-state tuition.

Check site for more details.

Requirements: Top Applicants.

Application Deadline: December 1

Application link: https://admissions.uic.edu/undergraduate/requirements-deadlines/deadlines/priority-scholarship-date

4 Monmouth College

Location: Monmouth, Illinois
Setting: Rural (112 Acres)
Undergraduate Enrollment: 753
Type: Private

William J. and Beverly Goldsborough scholarship: Awards Full tuition.

Requirements: A minimum 3.6 cumulative high school GPA. Check site for more details.

Admiral's Scholarship: Awards Full tuition plus $5,000 educational enrichment fund.

P.S: Recipients are required to participate in the James and Sybil Stockdale Fellows Program.
Requirements: A minimum 3.6 cumulative high school GPA.

Trustees' Scholarship: Awards Full tuition.
Requirements: A minimum 3.6 cumulative high school GPA.

Application Deadline: November 1

Application link:
https://www.monmouthcollege.edu/offices/student-financial-planning/types-of-aid/scholarships/

5 Quincy University

Location: Quincy, Illinois
Setting: City (70 Acres)
Undergraduate Enrollment: 1,052
Type: Private

Quincy University Presidential Scholarship: Awards Full tuition.

Requirements: A minimum ACT Score of 26 or SAT score of 1230 | A minimum high school GPA of 3.4 (on a 4.0 scale)

Application Deadline: January 10

Application link:
https://www.quincy.edu/admissions/financial-aid-and-tuition/scholarships/

6 Illinois State University

Location: Normal, Illinois
Setting: Urban (1,180 Acres)
Undergraduate Enrollment: 17,674
Type: Public

McLean County Full Tuition Scholarship: Awards Full tuition.

Eligibility: This scholarship is awarded to new freshmen from **McLean County** for demonstrating leadership, service, and commitment to their community | Top applicants.

Application Deadline: February 1

Application link:
https://illinoisstate.edu/admissions/scholarships/mclean-county/

7 Loyola University, Chicago

Location: Chicago, Illinois
Setting: City (105 Acres)
Undergraduate Enrollment: 11,819
Type: Private

Ignatian Scholarship: Awards Full tuition.

P.S: The Ignatian Scholarship is an invite-only full tuition scholarship.

Requirements: Top applicants.

Cristo Rey Scholars Program: Awards Full tuition.

Requirements: Top applicants.

Eligibility: This scholarship is awarded to students attending Cristo Rey Network schools in the United States.

Check site for more details:
https://www.luc.edu/undergrad/featurecontent/canvases/costandvalue/

National Merit/National Achievement Finalists: Awards Full tuition.

Eligibility: This scholarship is awarded to students who have been named National Merit/National Achievement finalists by the National Merit Corporation.

Check site for more details.

Application Deadline: December 1

Application link:
https://www.luc.edu/finaid/scholarships/undergraduate/

8

Eureka College

Location: Eureka, Illinois
Setting: Rural (65 Acres)
Undergraduate Enrollment: 476
Type: Private

Ronald W. Reagan Leadership Program: Awards Full tuition, two on-site mentorships with prominent leaders plus stipends to cover the program's travel and mentoring opportunities. Learn more: https://www.eureka.edu/ronald-reagan-leadership-program

Requirements: A minimum cumulative high school GPA of 3.0 (on a 4.0 scale) | Complete the two required essay prompts | Submit a resume along with two references.

Steven W. Rigazio Scholarship: Awards Full tuition.

P.S: This scholarship is awarded to a student who completes his/her second year at Illinois Valley Community College and transfers to Eureka College to pursue their baccalaureate degree.

Requirements: Top applicants.

Check site for more details…

The Uniquely Eureka Promise: This promise scholarship is designed to cover the remaining tuition charge for in-state students who graduated from specific Illinois high schools.

Out of state students are also considered for this award.

Requirements: A minimum 3.0 cumulative high school GPA.

Check site for more details.

Application Deadline: January 25

Application link: https://www.eureka.edu/admissions-and-financial-aid/scholarships-awards-and-veteran-benefits/scholarships-and-awards

9

Millikin University

Location: Decatur, Illinois
Setting: City (75 Acres)
Undergraduate Enrollment: 1,812
Type: Private

Presidential Scholarship: Awards Full tuition.

P.S: This award is for the best of the best.

Requirements: 3.5+ GPA (on a 4.0 scale)

Foley music Business Scholarship: Awards Full tuition.

P.S: This scholarship is awarded to students with demonstrated financial need who is majoring in music business.

Requirements: Top applicants.

The Amati String Scholarship: Awards Full tuition.

P.S: This scholarship is awarded to exceptionally talented string students in the School of Music.

Application Deadline: January 15

Application link: https://millikin.edu/scholarships

10 Illinois Wesleyan University

Location: Bloomington, Illinois
Setting: Suburban (82 Acres)
Undergraduate Enrollment: 1,653
Type: Private

President's Scholarships: Awards Full tuition (***to highly qualified international students***)

Requirements: Top Applicants.

Application Deadline: February 15

Application link:
https://www.iwu.edu/financial-aid/grants/SG_Types.html

11 Olivet Nazarene University

Location: Bourbonnais, Illinois
Setting: Suburban (275 Acres)
Undergraduate Enrollment: 2,643
Type: Private

Army ROTC: Award covers full tuition and mandatory fees plus a $300 - $500 monthly stipend and an annual allowance of $1,200 for books and miscellaneous fees.

Check site for more details.

Requirements: Top Applicants.

Application link:
https://www.olivet.edu/scholarships

12 Rockford University

Location: Rockford, Illinois
Setting: City (130 Acres)
Undergraduate Enrollment: 987
Type: Private

Charles & Dianna Colman Scholarship: Awards Full tuition.

Requirements: A minimum cumulative high school GPA of 3.75

Application Deadline: February 1

Application link:
https://www.rockford.edu/admission/financialaid/programs/

13

Illinois Institute of Technology

Location: Chicago, Illinois
Setting: Urban (120 Acres)
Undergraduate Enrollment: 2,998
Type: Private

Camras Scholars Program: This scholarship program awards full tuition for four (4)/five (5) years.

Requirements: Satisfy very high selection standards and demonstrate outstanding academics, involvement in extracurricular activities, and dedication to leadership.

Be a United States Citizen or permanent resident.

M.A. And Lila Self Leadership Scholarship:

Academy Scholarship: This scholarship program awards full tuition for four(4)/five(5) years.

Requirements: View scholarship page for detailed information.

Application Deadline: February 15

Crown Scholarship: This scholarship program awards full tuition for five (5) years (College of Architecture Only)

Requirements:

✓ Outstanding academic achievement

✓ Excelent artistic skills in frehand drawing

✓ Be a United States Citizen or permanent resident.

Application Deadline: November 15

Application link: https://www.iit.edu/admissions-aid/tuition-and-aid/scholarships/first-year-student-scholarships

1 University of Indiana

Location: Bloomington, Indiana
Setting: City (1,953 Acres)
Undergraduate Enrollment: 34,253
Type: Public

Adam W. Herbert Presidential Scholars Program: Awards a scholarship, a technology stipend, and a study abroad stipend.

Requirements: Check site for more details.

Application Deadline: November 1

Application link: https://scholarships.indiana.edu/future-scholars/index.html

2 University of Notre Dame

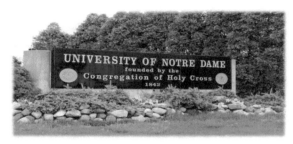

Location: Notre Dame, Indiana
Setting: Suburban (1,265 Acres)
Undergraduate Enrollment: 8,973
Type: Private

Notre Dame Stamps Scholars: Full tuition and fees for up to four years, books, personal expenses and transportation. Plus enrichment funds.

Requirements: Top Applicants.

Application Deadline: November 1

Application link: https://scholars.nd.edu/awards/list-of-awards/

3 Ball State University

Location: Muncie, Indiana
Setting: Suburban (1,180 Acres)
Undergraduate Enrollment: 13,916
Type: Public

Dr. T.M. Anderson Scholarship: Awards Full in-state tuition and required fees to a new Honors College student pursuing a major in history or a teaching major with a primary concentration in U.S. history.

P.S: Recipients do not need to be residents of Indiana.

Requirements: Top Applicants.

Deborah S Wehman Scholarship: Awards Full tuition.

O. L. Strong Memorial Scholarship: Awards Full in-sate tuition.

Requirements: Top Applicants.

Application Deadline: January 6

Application link: https://www.bsu.edu/academics/collegesanddepartments/honorscollege/admissions-and-financial-aid/scholarships

4 Earlham College

Location: Richmond, Indiana
Setting: City (800 Acres)
Undergraduate Enrollment: 658
Type: Private

Davis UWC Scholars Program: Awards range from partial scholarships to 50% tuition, as well as a $20,000-$25,000 Davis Grant which sums up to the full cost of tuition. In addition, a select number of students qualify for full awards which cover the costs of tuition, fees, room and board.

Requirements: Applicants should be graduates of the United World College

Check site for more details.

Application Deadline: December 1

Application link: https://earlham.edu/cost-affordability/types-of-aid/scholarships/

5

Trine University

Location: Angola, Indiana
Setting: Rural (400 Acres)
Undergraduate Enrollment: 3,811
Type: Private

Bateman Kolb Scholarship: Awards Full tuition.

Requirements: 3.9 (on a 4.0 scale) High school GPA | SAT 1310 (R+M) / ACT 26

Air Force ROTC Scholarship Program: Awards range from 18,000/year up to full tuition.

Application Deadline: March 5

Application link: https://www.trine.edu/admission-aid/tuition-aid/types-of-aid/competitive-scholarships.aspx

6 Marian University

Location: Indianapolis, Indiana
Setting: Suburban (120 Acres)
Undergraduate Enrollment: 2,980
Type: Private

Saint Mary Academic Scholarship: Awards full tuition.

Requirements: 3.90+ High school GPA.

21st Century Scholars Tuition Scholarship:

Awards full tuition and fees.

Eligibility: *Indiana Resident's*

Requirements: Top Applicants.

Athletic Award: Amount ranges from partial to full tuition.

P.S: Students selected for athletic scholarships are evaluated based on their athletic abilities and their potential to make a positive team contribution.

Requirements: Top Applicants.

Application Deadline: November 15

Application link:
https://www.marian.edu/admissions/financial-aid-at-marian-university/freshman-scholarships

7 Franklin College

Location: Franklin, Indiana
Setting: Suburban (207 Acres)
Undergraduate Enrollment: 899
Type: Private

Ben Franklin Scholars Program: Awards up full tuition.

Requirements: A minimum 3.9 cumulative high school GPA (on a 4.0 scale) | 1320+ SAT/ 28+ ACT

National Pulliam Journalism Scholarship: Awards full tuition.

P.S: Applicant must be interested in studying journalism | Students must submit a completed application and essay on or before November 15.

Application Deadline: December 1

Application link:
https://franklincollege.edu/admissions/financial-aid/types-financial-aid/scholarships-overview/

Grace College

8

Location: Winona Lake, Indiana
Setting: Rural (150 Acres)
Undergraduate Enrollment: 1,587
Type: Private

President's Scholarships: Awards Full tuition.

Requirements: A minimum 3.75 cumulative high school GPA | Top 20% class rank | Score 1260 SAT or 27 ACT

Indiana Low Income Plan: Awards Full tuition.

Eligibility: Applicant must be an *Indiana Resident* | Must complete the FAFSA by the Indiana state deadline of April 15 | Expected Family Contribution (EFC) of 0 to $1500 as calculated by the FASFA. Generally, parental income below $60,000 qualifies.

21st Century Scholars Tuition Scholarship: Awards Full tuition.

Eligibility: Applicant must be a 21st Century Scholar.

Check site for more details.

Application Deadline: October 1

Application link:
https://www.grace.edu/admissions/undergraduate/financial-aid-scholarships/scholarships-and-grants/

Hanover College

9

Location: Hanover, Indiana
Setting: Rural (640 Acres)
Undergraduate Enrollment: 1,004
Type: Private

Pell Promise Award: Awards Full tuition.

P.S: This Award covers full tuition for all admitted Indiana students who file the FAFSA by April 15

Requirements: Top applicants.

Lilly Scholars Promise: Awards Full tuition, required fees and book stipend for 4 years.

Eligibility: *Indiana Resident's.*

Requirements: Top applicants.

Application Deadline: February 15

Application link:
https://www.hanover.edu/admission/financialaid/

10 Goshen College

Location: Goshen, Indiana
Setting: City (135 Acres)
Undergraduate Enrollment: 749
Type: Private

President's Leadership Award: Awards Full tuition.

P.S: This scholarship requires an application, a personal experience portfolio (essay questions), and a video.

Requirements: A minimum high school cumulative GPA of 3.85 (on a 4.0 scale) | Score at least 1340 on the SAT **or** at least 29 on the ACT

Check site for more details.

Dream Award: Awards Full tuition.

P.S: This scholarship requires an application, a personal experience portfolio (essay questions), and a video.

Requirements: A minimum high school cumulative GPA of 3.0 (on a 4.0 scale) | Score at least 970 on the SAT **or** at least 18 on the ACT.

Application Deadline: November 15

Application link:
https://www.goshen.edu/financial-aid/scholarships/achievement/

11 Saint Mary of the Woods College

Location: Saint Mary-of-the-Woods, Indiana
Setting: Rural (227 Acres)
Undergraduate Enrollment: 793
Type: Private

Saint Mother Theodore Guerin Scholarship: Awards up to Full tuition and each winner will receive an iPad.

Requirements: Top applicants.

Center for Leadership Development (CLD): Awards Full tuition.

Eligibility: Applicants must complete the following CLD programs: Self-Discovery/Career-Exploration Project, Emerging Scholars Program, and College Prep Summer Program.

Post-9/11 GI Bill/Yellow Ribbon Program: Award covers the total cost of tuition and fees.

P.S: Qualifications determined by the Department of Veteran Affairs as determined by the Post 9/11 GI Bill and Yellow Ribbon Program requirements.

Check site for more details.

SMWC Musician of Promise Scholarship: Awards up to full tuition.

Application Deadline: January 22

Application link: https://www.smwc.edu/offices-resources/offices/financial-aid/scholarships-and-grants/campus-scholarships/

12

University of Indianapolis

Location: Indianapolis, Indiana
Setting: Urban (65 Acres)
Undergraduate Enrollment: 4,063
Type: Private

Presidential Scholarship: Awards up to full tuition.

Requirements: Top applicants.

R.B. Annis Engineering Scholarship: Awards Full tuition.

Eligibility: Top Dean Scholars Majoring in Engineering invited to on-campus competition.

P.S: Applicants must apply for admission by December 15

School of Education Scholarship: Awards range from $100 – Full tuition.

Requirements: Top applicants.

UIndy Diversity in Education Teaching Scholarship: Awards up to full tuition and $250 per semester ($500 total) book stipend.

P.S: Award based on demonstrated financial need | Students from underrepresented populations are encouraged to apply | Submit the Scholarship application by February 15 for priority consideration.

University of Indianapolis Freedom Award: Awards up to full tuition.

Eligibility: Applicant must be eligible for full Post 9/11 Veterans benefits and the Yellow Ribbon Program.

Discovery Award: Awards up to full tuition.

Eligibility: Applicant must be designated as a 21st Century Scholar through the State Commission as documented by the high school guidance counselor.

Promise Award: Awards up to full tuition.

Eligibility: *Indiana students* who are eligible for the Frank O'Bannon Award and who have maximum need may receive the award | Applicant must be designated as a Frank O'Bannon Award recipient by the Indiana Commission for Higher Education.

Application Deadline: February 15

Application link: https://www.uindy.edu/financial-aid/scholarships

1 Grand View University

Location: Des Moines, Iowa
Setting: Urban (25 Acres)
Undergraduate Enrollment: 1,694
Type: Private

Presidential Scholarship: Awards full tuition and an additional $5,000 award.

P.S: This scholarship is only available to Presidential Scholarship recipients.

Requirements: Top applicants.

Presidential Scholarship level may compete for full tuition and additional $5,000 awards at **scholarship days**: https://www.grandview.edu/admissions/financial-aid/scholarships-grants/scholarship-day

Application Deadline: December 1

Application link: https://www.grandview.edu/admissions/financial-aid/scholarships-grants

2 Drake University

Location: Des Moines, Iowa
Setting: City (150 Acres)
Undergraduate Enrollment: 2,902
Type: Private

Physics Scholarship: Awards full tuition.

P.S: Summer tuit tuition and fall/spring tuition overload charges (for enrollment exceeding 18 credits) are not covered.

Eligibility: This scholarship is offered annually to an incoming first-time college student majoring in Physics | Top applicants.

Drake Opportunity Scholarship: Awards full tuition (*to Syrian students*)

P.S: Summer tuit tuition and fall/spring tuition overload charges (for enrollment exceeding 18 credits) are not covered.

Eligibility: Top applicants.

Application Deadline: March 1

Application link: https://www.drake.edu/finaid/scholarships/

3 Graceland University

Location: Lamoni, Iowa
Setting: Rural (170 Acres)
Undergraduate Enrollment: 956
Type: Private

Prestigious Honors Scholarship: Awards Full tuition.

Requirements: A minimum high school cumulative GPA of 3.75 | Minimum SAT composite score of 1280 **or** at least 27 on the ACT.

Founders Scholarship: The Founders Scholarship will supplement other gift aid until the student's percentage of need, as calculated, has been met.

Eligibility: Applicant must demonstrate financial need.

Application Deadline: January 1

Application link:
https://www.graceland.edu/admissions-aid/tuition-financial-aid/scholarships-financial-aid/scholarships/

4 Briar Cliff University

Location: Sioux City, Iowa
Setting: City (70 Acres)
Undergraduate Enrollment: 766
Type: Private

Presidential Scholarship: Awards Full tuition.

Requirements: A minimum high school GPA of 3.75 | Applicants must provide two letter(s) of recommendation that describe strengths, weaknesses and characteristics that would judge the applicant's ability to succeed, be involved, and become a leader at Briar Cliff University.

P.S: Applicants must apply by the first week of December in the year prior.

Check site for more details.

Application Deadline: January 28

Application link:
https://www.briarcliff.edu/future-chargers/tuition-and-aid/scholarships

5

Coe College

Location: Cedar Rapids, Iowa
Setting: City (65 Acres)
Undergraduate Enrollment: 1,371
Type: Private

Distinguished Trustee Scholarship: Awards Full tuition.

Requirements: Top applicants.

Diversity Leadership Scholarship: Awards Full tuition.

Eligibility: Open to prospective students who are U.S. citizens, permanent residents or undocumented residents, from broadly diverse backgrounds.

Requirements: Top applicants.

Sustainability Scholarship: Awards Full tuition.

Eligibility: Open to prospective students who have a passion for the environment, creating sustainable practices and reducing our carbon footprint on the world.

P.S: No ACT/SAT score required to apply.

Requirements: Top applicants.

Marshall Music Scholarship: Awards Full tuition.

Eligibility: Open to prospective students who have the motivation and background necessary to pursue the Bachelor of Music degree.

P.S: No ACT/SAT score required to apply.

Requirements: Top applicants.

National Merit & Achievement: Awards up to full tuition.

Eligibility: This scholarship is awarded to National Merit and National Achievement Finalists.

Global Leadership Scholarship: Awards Full tuition **(to international students)**

Eligibility: Applicant must be a non-U.S. citizen attending high school outside of the U.S.

P.S: Application deadline is February 1

Requirements: Top applicants.

Application Deadline: January 4

Application link:
https://www.coe.edu/admission/first-year-students/scholarships-awards

6 Central College

Location: Pella, Iowa
Setting: Rural (200 Acres)
Undergraduate Enrollment: 1,139
Type: Private

Kuyper Scholarships & Rolscreen Scholarships: Awards Full tuition.

Requirements: Top applicants.

P.S: These scholarships are the most prestigious awards granted at Central College. Recipients will be chosen after all the Scholar Days are completed.

Application Deadline: January 15

Application link:
https://central.edu/financial-aid/scholarships-awards/

7 Mount Mercy University

Location: Cedar Rapids, Iowa
Setting: Suburban (45 Acres)
Undergraduate Enrollment: 1,290
Type: Private

Sister Mary lidephonse Holland Scholarship: Awards Full tuition.

P.S: Scholarship is awarded from participation in Scholarship Day.

Requirements: A minimum 26 ACT (SAT 1230) composite score and a 3.7 cumulative GPA.

Catherine McAuley Scholarship: Awards Full tuition

P.S: This is a Need-based free tuition award. Applicant must be Iowa resident and graduate from an Iowa high school.

Requirements: Top applicants.

Application Deadline: March 1

Application link:
https://www.mtmercy.edu/admissions-aid/undergraduate/scholarships/index

8 University of Iowa

Location: Iowa City, Iowa
Setting: City (2,122 Acres)
Undergraduate Enrollment: 21,608
Type: Public

Presidential Scholarship: The value of the award covers full tuition and fees (*Iowa Resident's*)

Requirements: A minimum 3.80 cumulative high school GPA (weighted or unweighted) | 33+ ACT or an equivalent SAT score.

Mark Shapiro Sports Journalism Scholarship: Awards $35,000 (This covers the cost of tuition and fees for out-of-state students)

P.S: This scholarship is awarded to an incoming freshman in the University of Iowa School of Journalism and Mass Communication (SJMC) who is interested in pursuing a career in sports journalism/communication. The incoming freshman student should be a graduate of a high school outside of Iowa.

Requirements: Top applicants.

Application Deadline: March 1

Application link: https://tippie.uiowa.edu/undergraduate/tuition-aid

9 Simpson College

Location: Indianola, Iowa
Setting: Suburban (85 Acres)
Undergraduate Enrollment: 1,172
Type: Private

Cowles Fellowship: Award range from $29,000 to full tuition plus a travel stipend to be used for international/domestic travel or internship study to enhance the student's educational experience.

P.S: Candidates must possess extraordinary academic ability and potential as evidenced by high school performance, including standardized test scores.

Requirements: Top applicants.

Trustee Scholarship: Award range from ½ to full tuition.

Requirements: Top applicants.

Application Deadline: February 1

Application link: https://simpson.edu/admission-aid/tuition-aid/scholarships-grants-awards/first-year-scholarships-and-awards

10
Iowa Wesleyan University

Location: Mount Pleasant, Iowa
Setting: Rural (60 Acres)
Undergraduate Enrollment: 748
Type: Private

Presidential Scholarship: Awards Full tuition.

Requirements: High school GPA of 3.5 or higher | A minimum 25 ACT (SAT 1200) score.

P.S: Presidential Scholar competitors are required to visit campus to complete an essay and interview on-campus from November 1 through February 1.

Application Deadline: Check site for more details.

Application link: https://www.iw.edu/institutional-aid/

11
Saint Ambrose University

Location: Davenport, Iowa
Setting: City (113 Acres)
Undergraduate Enrollment: 2,968
Type: Private

Ambrose Advantage: Awards Full tuition.

P.S: Applicant must be an Iowa resident | Federal Pell Grant eligible.

Requirements: A minimum 2.8 high school GPA (unweighted)

Application Deadline: Check site for more details.

Application link: https://www.sau.edu/admissions-and-aid/first-year

12 Wartburg College

Location: Waverly, Iowa
Setting: Rural (170 Acres)
Undergraduate Enrollment: 1,513
Type: Private

McElroy/Slife Scholarship: Awards Full tuition.

P.S: Preference to students from the Waterloo/Cedar Falls, Iowa, area.

Requirements: Applicant is required to write a 250-500 word essay on "How you would benefit from a Wartburg education" | Top applicants.

Check site for more details.

Tuition Exchange Program for Imports: Awards up to Full tuition.

P.S: Dependents of employees at other higher education institutions may qualify for the tuition exchange program.

Application Deadline: March 15

Application link:
https://www.wartburg.edu/scholarships/

13 Iowa State University

Location: Ames, Iowa
Setting: City (1,813 Acres)
Undergraduate Enrollment: 25,808
Type: Public

George Washington Carver Program: Awards Full tuition.

Requirements: Applicants must fulfill one of these requirements to be eligible for this scholarship – Have a 3.70 cumulative high school GPA | A minimum SAT score of 1160 (Reading and Writing + Math) OR A minimum ACT composite score of 24.

Application Deadline: January 10

Learn more:
https://www.multicultural.dso.iastate.edu/programs/gwc?fbclid=IwAR01gcsGw3DPaVvS0XgC8R0Hbp_X20tmyhu5MZPW3ppZ7GlB5ZJXjln4qjl

Iowa Resident National Merit Full tuition Scholarship: Awards Full tuition to National Merit Scholars.

Application link:
https://www.admissions.iastate.edu/scholarships/freshman/ia

1

University of Kansas

Location: Lawrence, Kansas
Setting: City (1,000 Acres)
Undergraduate Enrollment: 19,158
Type: Public

International Excellence Award: Award covers up to full tuition.

P.S: This scholarship is awarded to *international student's.*

Requirements: A minimum 3.5 cumulative high school GPA | Top applicants.

KU Pell Advantage: Award covers up to full tuition.

Eligibility: Applicant must be a *Kansas Resident* | Must file the FAFSA by Feb. 1 each year and be Pell Grant eligible.

Requirements: A minimum 3.25 cumulative high school GPA | 22 ACT or 1100 SAT

Check site for more details.

Application Deadline: March 1

Application link: https://admissions.ku.edu/afford/scholarships

Fort Hays State University

Location: Hays, Kansas
Setting: Rural (200 Acres)
Undergraduate Enrollment: 11,404
Type: Public

RGK Scholarship: Awards $10,000. This covers the value for in-state tuition.

P.S: The application should be accompanied by a letter of introduction from the applicant explaining his/her education and career goals, as well as a letter of recommendation.

Requirements: Top applicants.

Jack and Peggy McCullick Scholarship: Awards $5,450. This covers the value for in-state tuition.

P.S: This scholarship is open to all **College of Business and Entrepreneurship majors** in CIS, accounting and finance who will be classified as juniors or seniors by fall semester.

Requirements: A minimum 3.5 cumulative high school GPA | Top applicants.

Earl O and Winona M Field Athletic Scholarship: Awards $8,000. This covers the value for in-state tuition.

Ed and Donna Stehno Endowed Scholarship: Awards $7,500. This covers the value for in-state tuition.

P.S: The recipient of this scholarship(s) must be a student athlete at Fort Hays State University.

Application Deadline: February 15

Application link: https://fhsu.academicworks.com/?page=1

3 Newman University

Location: Wichita, Kansas
Setting: Urban (61 Acres)
Undergraduate Enrollment: 1,577
Type: Private

St. John Henry Newman Scholarship: Awards Full tuition.

Requirements: Cumulative 3.9+ high school GPA | Super scored 29+ ACT OR Super scored 1330+ SAT.

Check site for more details.

Application Deadline: December 1

Application link: https://newmanu.edu/scholarships/fts

4 Ottawa University

Location: Ottawa, Kansas
Setting: Rural (64 Acres)
Undergraduate Enrollment: 692
Type: Private

Presidential Scholarship: Award covers up to full tuition.

Requirements: Top applicants.

High Achiever Scholarship: Award covers up to full tuition.

P.S: This scholarship is awarded to select senior students who are residents or attending a high school in **Surprise, Arizona**, and who excel academically and show engagement in extracurricular activities.

Requirements: A minimum cumulative high school GPA (unweighted) of 3.50 (4.0 scale) | A minimum ACT composite score of 25 or A minimum SAT composite score of 1200

Franklin County High Achiever Scholarship:

Award covers up to the full cost of tuition.

P.S: This scholarship is awarded to select graduates from a Franklin County (KS) High School who demonstrates academic achievement and community service.

Requirements: Top applicants.

Application Deadline: August 1

Application link: https://www.ottawa.edu/ouks/admissions/scholarships

5 Benedictine College

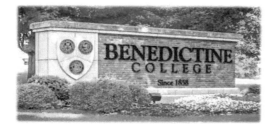

Location: Atchison, Kansas
Setting: Rural (120 Acres)
Undergraduate Enrollment: 2,205
Type: Private

National Merit Finalist Scholarships:

Awards Full tuition (*to National Merit Finalists and National Hispanic Merit Finalists.*)

Requirements: Top applicants.

Presidential Scholarships: Awards Full tuition.

Requirements: A minimum 27 ACT/1260 SAT | A non-weighted 3.5 cumulative high school GPA.

Check site for more details.

U.S. Army/Air Force ROTC Scholarships are also available.

Application Deadline: January 15

Application link:
https://www.benedictine.edu/admission/financial-aid/scholarships/index

6 Southwestern College

Location: Winfield, Kansas
Setting: Rural (85 Acres)
Undergraduate Enrollment: 1,164
Type: Private

Pillars Academic Scholarship: Awards Full tuition.

Requirements: Top Applicants

Moundbuilder Spirit Scholarship: Awards Full tuition. Requirements: Top Applicants.

Application Deadline: January 5

Application link:
https://www.sckans.edu/admissions/scholarships--grants/

7 Barclay College

Location: Haviland, Kansas
Setting: Rural (13 Acres)
Undergraduate Enrollment: 166
Type: Private

Full-Tuition Jubilee Scholarship: Awards Full tuition for four (4) years.

Requirement: Must be a full-time on-campus student with satisfactory academic performance.

Application Deadline: Contact Admission Office.

Application link:
https://www.barclaycollege.edu/admissions/campus/financial-assistance/

8 University of Saint Mary

Location: Leavenworth, Kansas
Setting: Rural (200 Acres)
Undergraduate Enrollment: 858
Type: Private

Full-Tuition Jubilee Scholarship: Awards Full tuition.

Requirements: A minimum 3.7 cumulative high school GPA or be ranked in the top 10 Percent of your graduating high school class | A minimum ACT score of 26 or SAT equivalent.

Application Deadline: December 1

Application link:
https://www.stmary.edu/scholarships

Bellarmine University

Location: Louisville, Kentucky
Setting: Urban (145 Acres)
Undergraduate Enrollment: 2,407
Type: Private

Bellarmine Fellow Award: Awards Full tuition plus a study abroad stipend and enrollment in Bellarmine's Honors Program.

Requirements: An essay with the topic "Describe an incident or situation in your life which piqued your intellectual curiosity" | A minimum SAT score of 1390/ACT 30 & 3.4 GPA.

Monsignor Horrigan Scholarship: Award covers tuition costs during the fall and spring semesters.

P.S: The Horrigan Scholarship is reserved for high-achieving students and receiving this award demonstrates the strength of a student's application.

The priority deadline to apply is February 1.

Requirements: Top applicants.

Whitney Young Scholarship Program: This award is combined with federal and state scholarships and grants (PELL, SEOG, CAP, KTG and KEES) to cover full Bellarmine tuition not including room and board or fees.

P.S: You must apply separately for this scholarship by February 1.

Check site for more details.

Requirements: Top applicants.

Application Deadline: February 1

Application link: bellarmine.edu/financial-aid/institutional/

2 Murray State University

Location: Murray, Kentucky
Setting: Rural (253 Acres)
Undergraduate Enrollment: 7,735
Type: Public

Trustee Scholarship: Awards Full tuition plus a $1,500 Stipend.

Requirements: 33-36 ACT (OR 1450-1600 SAT), and 3.70 – 4.00 GPA.

Kentucky GSP and GSA Scholarship: Awards Full tuition.

P.S: Applicant must be majoring in Art, Music or Theatre.

Requirements: A minimum 3.5 cumulative high school GPA | A minimum 25 ACT composite score.

The Murray State Promise Tuition Program is also available to Kentucky resident's.

Application Deadline: February 1

Application link: https://www.murraystate.edu/admissions/scholarships/newfreshmen.aspx

3 Transylvania University

Location: Lexington, Kentucky
Setting: Urban (46 Acres)
Undergraduate Enrollment: 971
Type: Private

William T. Young: Awards Full tuition and fees.

Eligibility: Students eligible for these Premier Scholarship awards will be selected based on application materials, academics, essays and an interview.

Requirements: Top applicants.

Application Deadline: December 1

Application link: https://www.transy.edu/financial-aid/scholarships-grants-aid/

4

Northern Kentucky University

Location: Highland Heights, Kentucky
Setting: Suburban (428 Acres)
Undergraduate Enrollment: 11,882
Type: Public

Presidential Scholarship: Awards Full tuition plus $6,000 for students living in NKU housing.

Requirements: 34+ ACT (OR 1490+ SAT), and 3.75+ Weighted HS GPA.

Kentucky Governor's Scholars Program (GSP): Awards up to Full tuition (to students who have participated in the Kentucky Governor's Scholars Program (GSP)

Kentucky Governor's School for the Arts Program (GSA): Awards up to Full tuition (to students who have participated in the Kentucky Governor's School for the Arts Program (GSA)

Kentucky Governor's School for Entrepreneurs Program (GSE): Awards up to Full tuition (to students who have participated in the Kentucky Governor's School for Entrepreneurs Program (GSE)

Requirements: A minimum 3.0 cumulative high school GPA | 24+ ACT/1160+ SAT.

William H. Greaves Scholarship: Awards Full in-state tuition and books. (Available to incoming freshmen students majoring in STEM disciplines)

Requirements: 25+ ACT | Applicant must rank in the top 25% of their high school class.

Check here for a detailed list of available scholarships in NKU:
https://inside.nku.edu/financialaid/programs/scholarships.html

Application Deadline: February 15

Application link: https://inside.nku.edu/financialaid/programs/scholarships/is-freshman/merit-based.html

5 Thomas More University

Location: Crestview Hills, Kentucky
Setting: Suburban (103 Acres)
Undergraduate Enrollment: 1,836
Type: Private

James Graham Brown Honors Program: Top 2 Candidates receive full tuition when combined with other institutional scholarships.

Requirements: 29+ ACT (OR 1130+ SAT OR 90 CLT), and 4.00 GPA.

Application Deadline: December 15

Information Systems Workship Program: Full Tuition Guarantee.

Requirements: Test optional 3.5 GPA (OR 3.0 GPA with required test scores (1130+ SAT | 23+ | 74 CLT)

Application Deadline: March 1

Application link:
https://www.thomasmore.edu/admissions/scholarships-financial-aid/scholarships/

6 Eastern Kentucky University

Location: Richmond, Kentucky
Setting: Rural (892 Acres)
Undergraduate Enrollment: 11,684
Type: Public

Merit Tier 1: Awards Full tuition (**to in-state students only**)

Requirements: Top applicants.

The "Colonel Commitment" Scholarship: Awards up to full tuition and fees.

Eligibility: This scholarship is awarded to Kentucky residents who are Pell Grant-eligible.

Requirements: A minimum high school GPA of 3.0

Check site for more details.

Governor's Scholar Program: Awards Full tuition.

P.S: Students who completed the Governor's Scholar Program will receive this full tuition award.

Requirements: An ACT composite score from 25 28 | 3.75+ high school GPA.

Application Deadline: August 1

Application link:
https://advantage.eku.edu/scholarships

7 Union College

Location: Barbourville, Kentucky
Setting: Rural (100 Acres)
Undergraduate Enrollment: 945
Type: Private

Merit Scholarships: Awards range from $15,000 up to the full cost of tuition.

Requirements: A minimum high school GPA of 2.0 | A minimum ACT composite score of 24.

U|GRAD Program: This program provides all first-time freshmen the opportunity to earn a full-tuition scholarship for the last semester of their senior year.

Application link:
https://www.unionky.edu/admissions-aid/undergraduate/union-distinction

8 Campbellsville University

Location: Campbellsville, Kentucky
Setting: Rural (95 Acres)
Undergraduate Enrollment: 5,880
Type: Private

Presidential Scholarship: Awards Full tuition.

Requirements: 30-32 on ACT/1980-2160 SAT and a 3.5 high school GPA.

Governor's Scholar Scholarship: Awards Full tuition.

P.S: This scholarship is awarded to students who have participated in the Kentucky Governor's Scholars Program. Application is required and will be awarded to students based on GPA, ACT/SAT, and quality and content of essay.

Requirements: A minimum 3.5 cumulative high school GPA | 25 ACT (1720 SAT)

Governor's Scholar for the Arts Scholarship: Awards Full tuition.

P.S: This scholarship is awarded to students who have participated in the Kentucky Governor's Scholars for the Arts Program.

Requirements: A minimum 3.0 cumulative high school GPA | 25 ACT and audition with the School of Music.

Application Deadline: November 1

Application link:
https://www.campbellsville.edu/admission-and-aid/scholarships-and-grants/

9

Lindsey Wilson College

Location: Columbia, Kentucky
Setting: Rural (200 Acres)
Undergraduate Enrollment: 1,750
Type: Private

Trustee Scholarship: Awards up to full tuition.

Requirements: A minimum high school GPA of 3.0 | A minimum ACT composite score of 30.

Walter S. Reuling Presidential Scholarship: Awards up to full tuition.

Requirements: Valedictorian (No other student(s) may share the same honor.) | A minimum high school GPA of 3.0 | A minimum ACT composite score of 24.

Award for Excellence: Awards up to full tuition.

Eligibility: Applicant must be a National Merit Semifinalists or National Achievement Semifinalists.

Requirements: A minimum high school GPA of 3.0 | A minimum ACT composite score of 24.

Kentucky Governor's Scholar Scholarship: Awards up to full tuition.

Eligibility: Kentucky Governor's Scholar, Kentucky Governor's School for the Arts, Kentucky Governor's School for Entrepreneurship.

Requirements: A minimum high school GPA of 3.0 | A minimum ACT composite score of 24.

Roger Scholar Scholarship: Awards up to full tuition.

Eligibility: Rogers Scholar.

Requirements: A minimum high school GPA of 3.0 | A minimum ACT composite score of 24.

Application Deadline: Check site for more details.

Application link: https://www.lindsey.edu/admissions/cost-and-financial-aid/Academic-Scholarships.cfm

10

Western Kentucky University

Location: Bowling Green, Kentucky
Setting: City (200 Acres)
Undergraduate Enrollment: 14,729
Type: Public

Cherry Presidential Scholarship

Cherry Presidential Scholarship: Awards up to $16,000 ($64,000 over a four year period)

Cherry Presidential Finalists: Receives an annual Award of up to $10,000 ($40,000 over a four year period)

This covers the total cost of tuition for in-state students.

Requirements: A minimum 29 ACT (1350 SAT) and a minimum 3.8 (unweighted) high school GPA.

Targeted Gatton & Craft Academy Graduates: Awards up to $10,000 ($40,000 over a four year period). This covers the total cost of tuition for in-state students.

Eligibility: This scholarship is awarded to Graduates of Gatton Academy or Craft Academy with a minimum 3.0 unweighted GPA.

The Hilltopper Guarantee is also available to Kentucky resident's. (Applicant must be a Pell grant recipient)

Application Deadline: January 4

Application link: https://www.wku.edu/financialaid/scholarships/freshmen-2122-academicyear.php

11

Kentucky State University

Location: Owensboro, Kentucky
Setting: City (916 Acres)
Undergraduate Enrollment: 2,135
Type: Private

Kentucky State University Offers a wide range of scholarships available to incoming freshmen.

Check site for more details:
https://www.kysu.edu/finance-and-administration/financial-aid/scholarships.php

There are Full ride Scholarship opportunities available in Kentucky State University.

Check our "Full Ride Scholarships book" for more details.

12

Kentucky Wesleyan College

Location: Owensboro, Kentucky
Setting: City (67 Acres)
Undergraduate Enrollment: 778
Type: Private

Wesleyan Scholars Scholarship Program

James Graham Brown Scholarship: Awards Full tuition.

Requirements: A minimum 3.5 cumulative high school GPA.

Application Deadline: March 1

Application link:
https://kwc.edu/admissions/financial-aid/scholarships/

University of Louisville

Location: Louisville, Kentucky
Setting: Urban (287 Acres)
Undergraduate Enrollment: 15,634
Type: Public

GSP, GSA, GSE Award/Gratton & Craft Academy/Rogers Scholars: Awards Full in-state tuition.

Requirements: A minimum 3.5 cumulative high school GPA | A minimum 31 ACT or 1390 SAT.

National Merit Finalist: Awards Full in-state tuition plus an $8,000 educational allowance to National Merit Finalist.

National Merit Semifinalist: Awards Full in-state tuition.

Requirements: A minimum 3.5 cumulative high school GPA.

Martin Luther King Scholars Program: Awards Full in-state tuition plus an $8,000 stipend to cover other university expenses.

Requirements: A minimum 3.5 cumulative high school GPA | A minimum ACT score of 26 or 1230 SAT.

P.S: This scholarship is awarded to Black/African American or Latino high school graduates from Kentucky or Southern Indiana.

Mentored Scholarships

Brown Fellows Program: Awards Full in-state tuition plus additional education allowance.

Requirements: A minimum 3.5 cumulative high school GPA | A minimum 29 ACT or 1330 SAT.

Grawemeyer Scholarship: Awards Full in-state tuition plus $8,000/year educational allowance.

Requirements: A minimum 3.5 cumulative high school GPA | A minimum 29 ACT or 1330 SAT.

McConnell Scholars: Awards Full tuition, plus educational allowance *(to Kentucky residents)*

Requirements: A minimum 3.5 cumulative high school GPA | Academic merit and leadership potential.

Application Deadline: January 15

Application link: https://louisville.edu/admissions/cost-aid/scholarships

1 Xavier University

Location: New Orleans, Louisiana
Setting: Urban (66 Acres)
Undergraduate Enrollment: 2,755
Type: Private

Presidential Scholarship: Full tuition and fees.

Saint Katharine Drexel Scholarship: Awards full tuition and fees to students who attend a Catholic high school within the United States and are the Valedictorian or Salutatorian of their high school graduating class.

Norman C. Francis Scholarship: Awards full tuition and fees to students who attend a public high school within Orleans or Jefferson Parishes and are the Valedictorian or Salutatorian of their high school graduating class.

There are some Specific Requirements for some of the listed scholarships.

Requirements: A minimum 3.3 GPA | 22 ACT/1140 SAT.

Application Deadline: January 31

Application link:
https://www.xula.edu/academic-scholarships/

2 Southeastern Louisiana University

Location: Hammond, Louisiana
Setting: Rural (365 Acres)
Undergraduate Enrollment: 12,487
Type: Public

Priority Scholarships: Awards Full tuition and fees.

Requirements: A minimum cumulative high school GPA of 3.5 | 27+ ACT

Application Deadline: January 15

Application link:
http://www.southeastern.edu/admin/fin_aid/scholarships/freshman-sch/index.html

3

Louisiana Christian University

Location: Pineville, Louisiana
Setting: Suburban (81 Acres)
Undergraduate Enrollment: 959
Type: Private

STEM to STEAM Scholarship: Awards Full tuition to select students from STEM accredited High Schools.

Requirements: A minimum 3.0 GPA | A minimum ACT score of 28 and 3 letters of recommendation.

P.S: Applicants must major in a Science/Arts program.

Jimmie Davis Scholarship: Awards full tuition.

Eligibility: Applicants must be PELL eligible, have a FASFA EFC of less than 1000, and be a TOPS recipient.

President's Leadership Award: Awards full tuition.

Requirements: A minimum 3.0 GPA | A minimum ACT score of 28.

P.S: Applicants must be recommended by Pastor or High School Principal, and demonstration of proven leadership on and off campus.

IMB Dependent Scholarship: Awards full tuition.

Eligibility: Spouses or unmarried children (23 years of age and younger) of active or retired International Mission Board missionaries are eligible for this scholarship.

Application Deadline: Check site for more details.

Application link: https://lcuniversity.edu/admissions/grants-scholarships/

4 Dillard University

Location: New Orleans, Louisiana
Setting: Urban (55 Acres)
Undergraduate Enrollment: 1,202
Type: Private

Presidential Scholarship: Awards Full tuition.

Requirements: A minimum 3.6 cumulative high school GPA (4.0 scale) | A minimum 25 ACT composite score or 1220 SAT combined score.

Application Deadline: March 15

Application link:
https://www.dillard.edu/financialaid/institutional-scholarships.php

5 Louisiana Tech University

Location: Ruston, Louisiana
Setting: Rural (2,277 Acres)
Undergraduate Enrollment: 10,053
Type: Public

Bulldog Out-of-State Scholarship: Awards Full tuition and fees (***to non-residents of Louisiana***)

Requirements: A minimum 2.5 cumulative high school GPA (on a 4.0 unweighted scale) | A minimum ACT score of 23 or 1130 SAT.

P.S: International students may be eligible for this scholarship if they meet the *specific requirements*:
https://www.latech.edu/documents/2018/05/buldog_out_of_state_international.pdf/

Application Deadline: January 5

Application link:
https://www.latech.edu/admissions/freshman-scholarships/

6 Tulane University of Louisiana

Location: New Orleans, Louisiana
Setting: Urban (110 Acres)
Undergraduate Enrollment: 8,610
Type: Private

Paul Tulane Award: Awards Full tuition.

Requirements: Top applicants.

P.S: Typical awardees are in the top 5% of their class and have a long resume of extra activities outside of just normal schoolwork.

Founders Scholarship: Awards Full tuition.

Requirements: Top applicants.

P.S: Typical awardees are in the top 10% of their class.

Dean' Honor Scholarships (DHS): Awards Full tuition.

Requirements: Top applicants.

P.S: To be considered, applicants must submit the Deans' Honor Scholarship Application, included with their application for admission, by December 15.

Application Deadline: January 15

Application link:
https://financialaid.tulane.edu/

7 University of Louisiana at Monroe

Location: Monroe, Louisiana
Setting: City (238 Acres)
Undergraduate Enrollment: 6,670
Type: Public

President's Distinguished: Awards up to $14,588. This amount covers the total cost of tuition and fees for in-state students.

P.S: Students with a 31-32 ACT score will be awarded a laptop, and students with a 33-36 ACT score will be awarded a laptop and a study abroad stipend (up to $4,500) sponsored by the President's Top Hawks Fund.

Check site for more details.

Requirements: A minimum ACT score of 27 or SAT equivalent.

Application Deadline: January 31

Application link:
https://www.ulm.edu/scholarships/freshmen.html

1 University of Southern Maine

Location: Portland, Maine
Setting: City (142 Acres)
Undergraduate Enrollment: 5,956
Type: Public

President's Scholar Award: Award range from $5,000 to $12,000. This amount covers the total cost of tuition and fees for in-state students.

Requirements: A minimum high school GPA of 3.5 (on a 4.0 scale)

Dirigo Scholar Award: Award range from $3,000 to $10,000. This amount covers the total cost of tuition for in-state students.

Requirements: A minimum high school GPA of 3.0 (on a 4.0 scale)

Application Deadline: April 1

Application link:
https://usm.maine.edu/scholarships

2 University of Maine

Location: Orono, Maine
Setting: Rural (660 Acres)
Undergraduate Enrollment: 9,447
Type: Public

Scholarship Programs for *Maine Residents*

Maine's Top Scholar: Awards Full tuition and fees.

P.S: Students are given the opportunity to participate in scholarly activity/research in their field and are invited to join the Honors College.

Requirements: Top applicants.

Scholarship Programs for *Out-of-State Residents*

Presidential Flagship: Award range from $20,000 up to Full tuition and fees.

Requirements: Top applicants.

P.S: *Semi-finalists with the National Merit Scholarship Corporation are eligible for the highest awards in this category, including: 100% Tuition and fees, up to 15 credits per semester, & standard room and board.*

Application Deadline: December 1

Application link:
https://go.umaine.edu/apply/scholarships/

1 University of Maryland

Location: College park, Maryland
Setting: Suburban (1,340 Acres)
Undergraduate Enrollment: 30,922
Type: Public

President's Scholarship: Award range from $2,000 to $12,500 per year. This amount covers the total cost of tuition and fees for in-state students.

Requirements: Top Applicants.

Application Deadline: December 1

Application link: https://www.admissions.umd.edu/finance/freshman-merit-scholarships

2 Mount St. Mary's University

Location: Emmitsburg, Maryland
Setting: Rural (1,500 Acres)
Undergraduate Enrollment: 2,055
Type: Private

Full-Tuition Founder's Scholarships: Awards Full tuition.

Requirements: A minimum 3.75 weighted high school GPA.

ROTC Scholarships: Awards Full tuition plus a monthly stipend.

Check site for more details.

Application Deadline: December 1

Application link: https://msmary.edu/admissions/financial-aid/first-year-student.html

3 Coppin State University

Location: Baltimore, Maryland
Setting: Urban (38 Acres)
Undergraduate Enrollment: 1,845
Type: Public

Eagle Honors Program Scholarship: Awards in-state tuition and fees.

Requirements: A minimum cumulative high school GPA of 3.0 | 1080 SAT/ACT 21

Application Deadline: October 1

Application link:
https://www.coppin.edu/tuition-and-aid/scholarships-and-scholars-programs

4 Stevenson University

Location: Baltimore County, Maryland
Setting: Suburban (145 Acres)
Undergraduate Enrollment: 2,979
Type: Private

Presidential Fellowship: Awards Full tuition.

Requirements: A minimum cumulative high school GPA of 3.7 (on a 4.0 scale) or a 93 on a 100-point scale (weighted or unweighted.)

Check site for more details.

Application Deadline: December 1

Application link:
https://www.stevenson.edu/admissions-aid/scholarships-financial-aid/types-of-aid/presidential-fellowship/

5

Loyola University Maryland

Location: Baltimore, Maryland
Setting: Urban (80 Acres)
Undergraduate Enrollment: 3,787
Type: Private

Marion Burk Knott Scholarship: Awards Full tuition.

P.S: This scholarship is awarded on a competitive basis to **Catholic students** residing in the **Archdiocese of Baltimore.**

Requirements: Top applicants.

Maryland Guaranteed Access Grant: The grant value for attendance at Maryland independent colleges and universities is equivalent to the cost of tuition, fees, room and board at the University of Maryland, College Park.

The matching GAPP award may consist of a combination of institutionally-funded need-based grants or merit scholarship assistance and may not exceed **Loyola's full cost of tuition and mandatory fees.**

Check site for more details.

Eligibility: Grant recipients must be legal residents of Maryland | A minimum high school GPA of 2.5 unweighted (on a 4.0 scale)

P.S: Any Maryland high school senior whose annual total family income is below 130 percent of the Federal poverty level is eligible to apply for this Guaranteed Access Grant.

Application Deadline: January 15

Application link: https://www.loyola.edu/department/financial-aid/undergraduate/programs/scholarships

6 McDaniel College

Location: Westminster, Maryland
Setting: Suburban (160 Acres)
Undergraduate Enrollment: 1,757
Type: Private

Presidential Scholarships: Award ranges from $1000 per year all the way up to full tuition.

Requirements: A minimum high school GPA of 3.85 | Top applicants.

Application Deadline: November 15

Application link:
https://www.mcdaniel.edu/admissions-cost/cost-financial-aid/types-financial-aid/mcdaniel-scholarships

7 Notre Dame of Maryland University

Location: Baltimore, Maryland
Setting: Suburban (60 Acres)
Undergraduate Enrollment: 807
Type: Private

Presidential Scholarships: Awards Full tuition.

Requirements: A minimum high school GPA of 3.5 (unweighted).

Eligibility: First-year Women's College Students.

Knott Scholarships: Awards up to Full tuition (to **Catholic students** residing within the **Archdiocese of Baltimore**)

Eligibility: First-year Women's College Students.

Application Deadline: February 15

Application link:
https://www.ndm.edu/admissions-aid/financial-aid/scholarships/institutional

8 Washington Adventist University

Location: Takoma Park, Maryland
Setting: Suburban (19 Acres)
Undergraduate Enrollment: 690
Type: Private

National Merit Finalist: Awards Full tuition for 4 years.

Eligibility: National Merit Finalists.

Check site for more details.

Application Deadline: February 1

Application link: https://www.wau.edu/admissions-aid/financial-aid/financial-assistance/scholarships/

9 Washington College

Location: Chestertown, Maryland
Setting: Rural (112 Acres)
Undergraduate Enrollment: 1,026
Type: Private

Presidential Scholarships

George Washington Signature Scholarship: Awards Full tuition.

P.S: *Presidential Fellows programs and scholarships are invitation only.*

Requirements: Top Applicants.

Application Deadline: November 15

Application link: https://www.washcoll.edu/admissions/admitted/available-scholarships.php

1 Bard College at Simon's Rock

Location: Great Barrington, Massachusetts

Setting: Rural (275 Acres)

Undergraduate Enrollment: 318

Type: Private

Elizabeth Blodgett Hall and Livingston Hall Scholarships: Awards Full tuition

Requirements: Top Applicants.

Application Deadline: November 1

Application link: https://simons-rock.edu/admission/tuition-and-financial-aid/scholarships.php

2 Worcester Polytechnic Institute

Location: Worcester, Massachusetts

Setting: City (95 Acres)

Undergraduate Enrollment: 5,224

Type: Private

Great Minds/CoMPASS Scholars Program: Awards up to the full cost of tuition and fees.

Requirements: Applicants must be Pell-eligible seniors attending a Worcester Public High School.

Application Deadline: February 1

Application link: https://www.wpi.edu/admissions/tuition-aid/types-of-aid/scholarships-grants/wpi-merit

3 Smith College

Location: Northampton, Massachusetts

Setting: Suburban (147 Acres)

Undergraduate Enrollment: 2,566

Type: Private

Springfield/Holyoke Partnership or the Greenfield/Holyoke Community College Scholarship: Awards Full tuition.

Learn more: https://www.smith.edu/admission-aid/financial-aid/transfer/merit

Requirements: Applicants must be students from public schools in Springfield and Holyoke, Massachusetts.

P.S: Transfer students are also eligible to apply

Application Deadline: November 15

Application link: https://www.smith.edu/admission-aid/financial-aid/first-year/merit

4 Massachusetts Maritime Academy

Location: Bourne, Massachusetts
Setting: Suburban (54 Acres)
Undergraduate Enrollment: 1,440
Type: Public

Admiral Maurice J Bresnahan Scholarship: Award covers the value for in-state tuition and fees.

Requirements: Top Applicants.

Captain Emery E Rice Scholarship: Award covers the value for in-state tuition and fees.

Requirements: Top Applicants.

P.S: Eligibility criteria can be obtained through the Admissions Office.

Application Deadline: February 1

Application link: https://www.maritime.edu/financial-aid/undergraduate-aid/awards

5 Bentley University

Location: Waltham, Massachusetts
Setting: Suburban (163 Acres)
Undergraduate Enrollment: 3,996
Type: Private

Bentley Trustee Scholarship: Awards Full tuition.

Requirements: Top Applicants.

Application Deadline: January 15

Application link: https://www.bentley.edu/undergraduate/tuition-financial-aid

6 Lesley University

Location: Cambridge, Massachusetts
Setting: City (5 Acres)
Undergraduate Enrollment: 1,861
Type: Private

Cambridge Rindge & Latin Merit Scholarship: Awards Full tuition.

Requirements: Applicants must be graduating from Massachusetts Cambridge Rindge and Latin High School | A minimum 3.0 HS GPA.

Boston Arts Academy Scholarship: Awards Full tuition.

Requirements: Applicant must be graduating from the Boston Arts Academy's Visual Arts program | A minimum 3.0 HS GPA.

P.S: Applicants for this scholarships would have to be nominated by their high school principal/guidance counsellor or the Boston Arts Academy.

Check site for more details.

Application Deadline: February 15

Application link:
https://lesley.edu/academics/guide-financial-aid-scholarships-undergraduate-first-year-and-transfer-students

7 University of Massachusetts - Lowell

Location: Lowell, Massachusetts
Setting: City (142 Acres)
Undergraduate Enrollment: 12,885
Type: Public

Chancellor's Scholarship: Awards Full tuition and mandatory fees.

Requirements: Top Applicants.

Dean's Scholarship Program: Annual award up to half of tuition and mandatory fees.

Requirements: Top Applicants.

Eligibility: These scholarships are awarded to **permanent residents of Massachusetts.**

Application Deadline: November 5

Application link:
https://www.uml.edu/thesolutioncenter/financial-aid/scholarships/freshmen.aspx

8 College of the Holy Cross

Location: Worcester, Massachusetts
Setting: Suburban (174 Acres)
Undergraduate Enrollment: 3,138
Type: Private

Ellis Scholarship: Awards Full tuition *(to Worcester residents)*

Eligibility: All applicants who reside in Worcester are considered.

Brooks Scholarship: Awards Full tuition *(to students who major in music)*

Learn more: https://www.holycross.edu/academics/programs/music/music-scholarships

Requirements: Top Applicants.

9 Westfield State University

Location: Westfield, Massachusetts
Setting: Suburban (256 Acres)
Undergraduate Enrollment: 4,239
Type: Public

Tsongas Scholarship: Awards Full tuition and fees *(to Massachusetts residents)*

Requirements: A minimum SAT score of 1360 or higher in Evidence-Based Reading & Writing and Math | 4.0 high school GPA on a 4.0 scale.

Application Deadline: January 1

Application link: https://www.westfield.ma.edu/cost-aid/scholarships

Bean Scholarship: Awards Full tuition.

Eligibility: Applicant must be a major in the *classics department*.

Requirements: Top Applicants.

P.S: International students from countries in which English is not spoken must submit their TOEFL scores no later than November 15.

Application Deadline: January 15

Application link: https://www.holycross.edu/how-aid-works/scholarships-grants

10 Babson College

Location: Wellesley, Massachusetts
Setting: Suburban (370 Acres)
Undergraduate Enrollment: 2,576
Type: Private

Weissman Scholarship: Awards Full tuition plus financial support for scholars to develop their unique talents and pursue their personal passions.

P.S: International students are eligible for this scholarship.

Requirements: Top Applicants.

Global Scholarship: Awards Full tuition **(to international students)**

Eligibility: Citizenship or permanent resident status from countries other than the U.S. or Canada.

11 Mount Holyoke College

Location: South Hadley, Massachusetts
Setting: Suburban (800 Acres)
Undergraduate Enrollment: 2,220
Type: Private

Mount Holyoke's Trustee Scholarship: Awards Full tuition.

Requirements: Top Applicants.

Application Deadline: November 15

Application link:
https://www.mtholyoke.edu/admission/apply-undergraduate-first-year/affording-mount-holyoke/financial-aid/types-financial-aid/non-need-based-scholarships-and-awards

Arthur M. Blank School for Entrepreneurial Leadership Scholarship: Awards Full tuition and other benefits.

Requirements: Applicant should possess an Entrepreneurial potential.

Diversity Leadership Award: Awards Full tuition.

Eligibility: Awarded to students with the greatest potential for leadership in creating a diverse community.

Enrico Dallas Scholarship: Awards Full tuition **(to Dallas residents)**

Requirements: Top Applicants.

Application Deadline: December 1

Application link: https://www.babson.edu/undergraduate/admission/tuition-and-financial-aid/merit-awards/

1 Davenport University

Location: Grand Rapids, Michigan
Setting: Suburban (77 Acres)
Undergraduate Enrollment: 4,325
Type: Private

Martin Luther King Inherit the Dream Scholarship: Awards up to Full tuition.

Requirements: A minimum 2.0 cumulative high school GPA.

Si Se Puede Cesar E. Chavez Scholarship: Awards up to Full tuition.

Requirements: A minimum 2.00 cumulative high school GPA.

Application Deadline: December 2

Application link: https://www.davenport.edu/financial-aid/scholarships

2 Eastern Michigan University

Location: Ypsilanti, Michigan
Setting: City (460 Acres)
Undergraduate Enrollment: 12,730
Type: Public

Education First Opportunity Scholarship (EFOS): Full tuition minus the Pell Grant.

Requirements: A minimum 3.0 cumulative high school GPA | Applicant must be eligible for the Pell Grant.

Application Deadline: February 15

Application link: https://www.emich.edu/finaid/types/scholarships/freshman.php

3 Michigan State University

Location: East Lansing, Michigan

Setting: Suburban (5,192 Acres)

Undergraduate Enrollment: 38,574

Type: Public

Distinguished Freshman Scholarship: Full tuition, fees for all four (4) years.

Requirements: Excellent Academic & extracurricular record

Application Deadline: Contact Admission Office.

Application link: https://admissions.msu.edu/cost-aid/scholarships/freshman/high-achieving

4 Andrews University

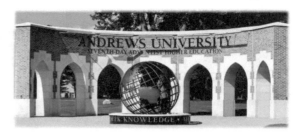

Location: Berrien Springs, Michigan

Setting: Rural (300 Acres)

Undergraduate Enrollment: 1,358

Type: Private

George Floyd Scholar Program: Awards up to Full tuition.

Requirements: Applicant must be eligible for a Pell Grant | Submission of an essay (minimum of 500 words)

National Merit/National Achievement Finalist Scholarship: Awards Full tuition to National Merit Finalists.

Learn more: https://bulletin.andrews.edu/content.php?catoid=11&navoid=1333

Application Deadline: June 1

Application link: https://www.andrews.edu/services/sfs/general_information/scholarships/index.html

5 University of Michigan - Dearborn

Location: Dearborn, Michigan
Setting: Suburban (202 Acres)
Undergraduate Enrollment: 6,355
Type: Public

Wade McCree Incentive Scholarship program: Awards Full tuition *(to qualified students from the Detroit or Southfield Public School System)*

Requirements: A minimum 3.0 cumulative high school GPA | A minimum composite ACT score of 21 or an SAT score of 1060.

Detroit Promise Scholarship: Awards Full tuition *(to qualified students who graduated from Detroit high schools)*

Requirements: A minimum 3.0 cumulative high school GPA | A minimum composite ACT score of 21 or an SAT score of 1060.

Check site for more details.

Application Deadline: December 1

Application link: https://umdearborn.edu/financial-aid/types-aid/scholarships

6 Saginaw Valley State University

Location: University Center, Michigan
Setting: Suburban (782 Acres)
Undergraduate Enrollment: 6,789
Type: Public

President's Scholarship: Awards Full tuition and selective mandatory fees.

Requirements: A minimum 3.9 cumulative high school GPA.

Application Deadline: December 1

Application link: https://www.svsu.edu/go/scholarships/

7 Oakland University

Location: Oakland County, Michigan
Setting: Suburban (1,444 Acres)
Undergraduate Enrollment: 13,771
Type: Public

Golden Grizzlies Tuition Guarantee: Awards up to Full tuition

View this pdf for more info: https://oakland.edu/Assets/Oakland/future students/files-and-documents/pdf/ADM-21253_GGTuitionGuaranteeFlier6%20(2). pdf

Requirements: Top Applicants.

Application Deadline: March 1

Application link: https://oakland.edu/futurestudents/scholar ships-cost-aid/

8 Siena Heights University

Location: Adrian, Michigan
Setting: Suburban (140 Acres)
Undergraduate Enrollment: 1,841
Type: Private

Trustee Scholarships: Awards up to Full tuition.

Requirements: A minimum 3.5 cumulative high school GPA.

Application Deadline: December 1

Application link: https://www.sienaheights.edu/residential-campus/financial-aid/scholarships-grants/

9 Wayne State University

Location: Detroit, Michigan
Setting: Urban (190 Acres)
Undergraduate Enrollment: 16,851
Type: Public

Wayne Access Tuition Pledge: Awards up to the full cost of tuition and standard fees at the in-state rate.

Eligibility: Applicant must demonstrate financial need by filing the Free Application for Federal Student Aid (FAFSA)

Heart of Detroit Tuition Pledge: Awards Full tuition and fees **(to Detroit residents)**

Eligibility: Applicant must graduate from any Detroit high school (public, private, charter, parochial, home school or GED program)

Check site for more details.

10 Olivet College

Location: Olivet, Michigan
Setting: Rural (56 Acres)
Undergraduate Enrollment: 968
Type: Private

Global Citizen Honors Program: Awards up to the full cost of tuition plus other benefits.

Requirements: Top Applicants.

Application Deadline: January 1

Application link:
https://www.olivetcollege.edu/academics/global-citizen-honors-program/

Born to Be a Warrior Tuition Pledge: Awards Full tuition and fees **(to eligible children of full-time Wayne State University employees)**

Requirements: A minimum 3.5 cumulative high school GPA.

P.S: International students will also be considered for this award.

President's Award for National Merit Scholarship Finalists: Awards $12,000 per year for four consecutive years, $5,000 per year towards on-campus room (double occupancy) and board for up to four years, One-time study abroad funding up to $2,500.

Application Deadline: December 1

Application link: https://wayne.edu/scholarships/freshmen

11 University of Detroit Mercy

Location: Detroit, Michigan
Setting: Urban (80 Acres)
Undergraduate Enrollment: 2,924
Type: Private

McNichols Puritan Lodge Community Counsel (MPLCC) Scholarship: Awards Full tuition.

Requirements: Top Applicants.

P.S: Applicants must be residents of the McNichols Puritan Lodge Community Counsel area, which include the boundaries of West McNichols on the north and Lodge Freeway to the south, with Livernois on the west and Log Cabin and Idaho Streets on the east.

Fellowships: Awards Full tuition plus other benefits.

Learn more:
https://lawschool.udmercy.edu/admissions/financial-aid/index.php

P.S: Fellowships are awarded to incoming students who have demonstrated excellence prior to **law school** through academics, leadership, professionalism, and service.

Application Deadline: February 1

Application link:
https://www.udmercy.edu/admission/financial-aid/sources/index.php

12 Adrian College

Location: Adrian, Michigan
Setting: City (132 Acres)
Undergraduate Enrollment: 1,805
Type: Private

Full Tuition Scholarships

The combination of the Full-Tuition Scholarship Award, State of Michigan grants or scholarships, Federal grants or scholarships, and private grants or scholarships will equal full tuition at Adrian College.
Check site for more details.

Application Deadline: August 1
Application link:
http://adrian.edu/admissions/financial-aid/tuition-scholarships/

13 Lake Superior State University

Location: Sault Ste. Marie, Michigan
Setting: Rural (115 Acres)
Undergraduate Enrollment: 1,812
Type: Public

Laker Gold Scholarship: Awards Full tuition.

Philip A Hart Scholarship: Awards Full tuition *(to Michigan resident's)*

Requirements: A minimum 3.5 cumulative high school GPA.

Application Deadline: December 15

Application link:
https://www.lssu.edu/financial-aid/types-of-aid/scholarships/2022-2023-incoming-freshmen-scholarships/

14 Rochester University

Location: Rochester Hills, Michigan
Setting: Suburban (76 Acres)
Undergraduate Enrollment: 1,087
Type: Private

Trustee Award: Awards Full tuition.

Requirements: A minimum 3.60 cumulative high school GPA (4.0 scale) | 1370+ SAT/ 30+ ACT

P.S: National Merit Scholar Semi-Finalists automatically receive this award.

Application Deadline: Check site for more details.

Application link:
https://rochesteru.edu/admissions/undergraduate-admissions/scholarship-opportunities/

15 Baker College

Location: Owosso, Michigan
Setting: Urban (53 Acres)
Undergraduate Enrollment: 7,606
Type: Private

Presidential Scholarship: Awards Full tuition.

Requirements: A minimum cumulative high school GPA of 3.8 (on a 4.0 scale) | 1390+ SAT score or 30+ ACT score.

Check site for more details.

Application Deadline: December 15

Application link:
https://www.baker.edu/admissions-and-aid/tuition-and-aid/scholarships/

16
Albion College

Location: Albion, Michigan
Setting: Suburban (574 Acres)
Undergraduate Enrollment: 1,523
Type: Private

Albion College Promise: Awards Full tuition and fees *(to Michigan residents)*

Eligibility: This Scholarship is awarded to Michigan families making under $65,000 annually.

Scholarships for Incoming **Students Residing in Michigan's Upper Peninsula**: Awards Full tuition to students residing in Michigan's Upper Peninsula.

Requirements: Top Applicants.

Application Deadline: December 1

Application link:
https://www.albion.edu/offices/financial-aid/aid-scholarships/scholarships/

17
Alma College

Location: Alma, Michigan
Setting: City (125 Acres)
Undergraduate Enrollment: 1,340
Type: Private

Performance Scholarships: Awards up to Full tuition.

Eligibility: Awarded to students demonstrating exemplary performance in art, dance, music (both vocal and instrumental), theatre and Scottish Arts.

Check site for more details.

Application Deadline: February 1

Application link;
https://www.alma.edu/admissions/financial-aid/grants-scholarships/alma-scholarships/

1 Bethel University

3900 Bethel Drive

Location: Saint Paul, Minnesota
Setting: Suburban (245 Acres)
Undergraduate Enrollment: 2,587
Type: Private

Arts & Humanities Scholarship: Full tuition or $10,000 awarded annually.

Requirements: A minimum 3.0 cumulative high school GPA (4.0 scale) | A minimum ACT score of 25, SAT score of 1200 | Applicant must be a U.S. citizen or permanent resident.

Check site for more details.

Bethel Physics & Engineering Scholarship: Awards two full-tuition and two $10,000 per year (to students planning to pursue a primary major in the **Department of Physics and Engineering**)

Requirements: A minimum 3.5 cumulative high school GPA (4.0 scale) | Applicant must be a U.S. citizen or permanent resident.

Application Deadline: January 15

Application link:
https://www.bethel.edu/undergrad/financial-aid/types/scholarships/

2 Hamline University

Location: Saint Paul, Minnesota
Setting: Urban (60 Acres)
Undergraduate Enrollment: 1,825
Type: Private

Fulford-Karp Physics Scholarship: Awards up to the full cost of tuition to students who demonstrate interest in pursuing a degree and aptitude in the **field of physics.**

Requirements: Top Applicants.

Application Deadline: February 1

Application link:
https://www.hamline.edu/admission-aid/financial-aid/grants-scholarships/first-year

3 University of Minnesota Morris

Location: Morris, Minnesota
Setting: Rural (130 Acres)
Undergraduate Enrollment: 1,286
Type: Public

Prairie Scholars: Awards Full tuition.

Requirements: Top Applicants.

National Merit Scholarships: Awards Full tuition.

Eligibility: Awarded to National Merit Finalists.

Application Deadline: December 15

Application link: https://morris.umn.edu/admissions/scholarships

4 University of Minnesota Twin Cities

Location: The Twin Cities of Minneapolis and Saint Paul, Minnesota
Setting: Urban (1,204 Acres)
Undergraduate Enrollment: 36,209
Type: Public

College of Science and Engineering

Robert K. Anderson Scholarship: Awards Full tuition.

Eligibility: Awarded to students from *High Schools in Crow Wing County.*

Requirements: Top Applicants.

Application Deadline: November 1

Application link: https://admissions.tc.umn.edu/cost-aid/scholarships

5 ## Bethany Lutheran College

Location: Mankato, Minnesota
Setting: City (50 Acres)
Undergraduate Enrollment: 781
Type: Private

Meyer Scholarship: Awards Full tuition.

Requirements: A minimum 3.6 cumulative high school GPA | A minimum ACT score of 26/ SAT score of 1240+

Aspire MN Grant: Awards up to Full tuition.

P.S: **Minnesota residents** who are eligible for the Minnesota State Grant and the Federal Pell Grant may qualify for the Aspire MN Grant. Together, these three grants **cover tuition in full**. Residential students who receive the Aspire MN Grant will also receive a discounted rate for room and board.

Requirements: A minimum 2.75 cumulative high school GPA.

Application Deadline: February 28

Application link: https://blc.edu/admissions/financial-aid/scholarships/academic-scholarships/

6 ## Concordia College

Location: Moorhead, Minnesota
Setting: Suburban (115 Acres)
Undergraduate Enrollment: 1,883
Type: Private

Act Six Leadership Scholarship: Awards Full tuition.

Learn more: https://www.concordiacollege.edu/tuition-aid/scholarships/concordia-scholarships/act-six-leadership-scholarship/

Requirements: Top Applicants.

P.S: Concordia announced that it would reset its tuition rate effective Fall 2021. This fall (2021) tuition is $27,500 for all new students.

Application Deadline: January 15

Application link: https://www.concordiacollege.edu/tuition-aid/scholarships/concordia-scholarships/

7 University of St. Thomas

Location: Saint Paul, Minnesota
Setting: Urban (78 Acres)
Undergraduate Enrollment: 6,067
Type: Private

Dease Scholarship Program: Awards Full tuition.

Requirements: Top Applicants.

Eligibility: Awarded to underrepresented domestic, first-generation students and/or graduates from urban high schools.

GHR Fellows Program: Awards Full tuition and required fees (to students pursuing *careers in business*)

Requirements: A minimum 3.7 cumulative high school GPA | Applicant must intend to major in business.

Schulze Innovation Scholarship: Awards Full tuition.

Requirements: A minimum 3.5 cumulative high school GPA | Applicant must intend to *major in Entrepreneurship.*

Application Deadline: January 8

Science, Mathematics & Engineering Scholarships: Awards two full-tuition scholarships and two $8,000/year Scholarships

Requirements: A minimum 3.5 cumulative high school GPA | Applicant must intend to *major in Science, Mathematics and/or Engineering field.*

Application Deadline: February 15

Application link: https://www.stthomas.edu/admissions/undergraduate/financial-aid/scholarships/future-students/index.html

8 The College of Saint Scholastica

Location: Duluth, Minnesota
Setting: Suburban (186 Acres)
Undergraduate Enrollment: 2,481
Type: Private

Sister Mary Rochefort Community Builder Scholarship: Awards Full tuition.

Requirements: A minimum 3.5 unweighted high school GPA | An ACT composite score of 24+ (or the SAT equivalent)

Application Deadline: March 1

Application link: https://www.css.edu/admissions-and-aid/financial-aid/scholarships-and-grants/

9 North Central University

Location: Minneapolis, Minnesota
Setting: Urban (9 Acres)
Undergraduate Enrollment: 950
Type: Private

Regent's Scholarship: Awards Full tuition.

Eligibility: Awarded to an applicant with an active membership and regular attendance at an Assemblies of God church.

Requirements: A minimum 3.5 cumulative high school GPA | A minimum ACT score of 30 (SAT score of 1320)

George Floyd Memorial Scholarship: Awards Full tuition.

Eligibility: Applicant must be of African American origin | Be a United States citizen.

Act Six Scholarship Program: Awards Full tuition.

Application Deadline: March 15

Application link: https://www.northcentral.edu/financial-aid/types-of-aid/grants-and-scholarships/

10 University of Northwestern – St. Paul

Location: Saint Paul, Minnesota
Setting: Suburban (107 Acres)
Undergraduate Enrollment: 3,289
Type: Private

Act Six Scholarship Program: Awards Full tuition and fees.

Application Deadline: February 1

Application link: https://unwsp.edu/admissions/financial-aid/unw-scholarships/

11 Gustavus Adolphus College

Location: St. Peter, Minnesota
Setting: Rural (340 Acres)
Undergraduate Enrollment: 2,247
Type: Private

National Merit College-Sponsored Scholarship

National Merit finalists will receive a *Full Tuition Scholarship.*

Application Deadline: November 1
Application link: https://gustavus.edu/admission/financial-aid/scholarships.php

1 Rust College

Location: Holly Springs, Mississippi
Setting: Rural (126 Acres)
Undergraduate Enrollment: 623
Type: Private

Presidential Scholarship: Awards $12,000, this covers the value for tuition and fees.

Requirements: A minimum 3.25 high school GPA.

Academic Dean Scholarship: Awards $10,000, this covers the value for tuition and fees.

Requirements: A minimum 3.0 high school GPA.

Application Deadline: December 1

Application link:
https://www.rustcollege.edu/prospective-students/financial-aid/scholarships/

2 Mississippi State University

Location: Starkville, Mississippi
Setting: Rural (4,200 Acres)
Undergraduate Enrollment: 18,584
Type: Public

Provost Scholarship Award: Awards Full tuition, a $4,000 scholarship for study abroad, a research grant of $1,500 for academic research and/or creative discovery, a one-summer optional tuition credit of $1,000 ($2,400 for non-resident) and one summer of free housing in Griffis Hall, an optional $750 travel grant to a conference (to be provided by Honors)

Requirements: A minimum 1330 SAT/ 30 ACT | A minimum 3.75 high school GPA.

Application Deadline: December 1

Application link:
https://www.honors.msstate.edu/scholarships/

3 University of Mississippi

Location: Oxford, Mississippi
Setting: Rural (3,693 Acres)
Undergraduate Enrollment: 16,092
Type: Public

University Foundation Scholarship

W. R. Newman Scholarship: Awards $10,000 per year. This covers the total cost of tuition and fees for in-state students.

Eligibility: Mississippi residents | Top Applicants.

Robert M. Carrier Scholarship: Awards $10,000 per year. This covers the total cost of tuition and fees for in-state students.

Eligibility: Mississippi residents | Top Applicants.

School of Business Administration Scholarships

Christine and Clarence Day Business Scholarship: Awards $10,000 per year. This covers the total cost of tuition and fees for in-state students.

Eligibility: Mississippi high-school graduates pursuing **business degrees** | Top Applicants.

Application Deadline: January 5

Application link:
https://finaid.olemiss.edu/scholarships/#12

4 University of Southern Mississippi

Location: Hattiesburg, Mississippi
Setting: Suburban (1,090 Acres)
Undergraduate Enrollment: 10,693
Type: Public

Presidential National Merit Semifinalist Scholarship: Awards Full tuition and fees.

Eligibility: National Merit Semifinalist.

Application Deadline: January 15

Application link:
https://catalog.usm.edu/content.php?catoid=9&navoid=515

5 Mississippi Valley State University

Location: Itta Bena, Mississippi
Setting: Rural (450 Acres)
Undergraduate Enrollment: 1,694
Type: Public

Vice President's Scholarship: Awards Full tuition, fees, and a book allowance of $300.

Requirements: A minimum 3.0 cumulative high school GPA | An ACT score of 22-23 (SAT equivalent)

Valedictorian/Salutatorian Academic Scholarship: Awards Full tuition, fees, and a book allowance of $200.

Eligibility: Awarded to freshmen who have attained the honor of being the Valedictorian or Salutatorian of the their high school graduating class.

University Scholarship: Award covers ½ tuition and fees and a book allowance of $200.

Requirements: A minimum 3.0 cumulative high school GPA | An ACT score of 20-21 (SAT equivalent)

Application Deadline: February 1

Application link:
https://www.mvsu.edu/prospective-students/scholarships

6 Millsaps College

Location: Jackson, Mississippi
Setting: City (100 Acres)
Undergraduate Enrollment: 697
Type: Private

Millsaps Yellow Ribbon Program: Awards Full tuition and fees *(to Veterans)*

P.S: The VA's Yellow Ribbon Program is a benefit in which Millsaps partners with the Department of Veterans Affairs to ensure that Yellow Ribbon 100% eligible recipients receive matching institutional funds to cover tuition and fees.

Check site for more details.

Application Deadline: March 1

Application link:
https://www.millsaps.edu/financial-aid/scholarships-grants-loans-students/

1 Maryville University

Location: St. Louis, Missouri
Setting: Suburban (130 Acres)
Undergraduate Enrollment: 5,684
Type: Private

Trustee Scholarship: Awards Full tuition.

Requirements: A minimum 3.75 cumulative high school GPA | 1290+ SAT / 27+ ACT

Melissa Brickey Scholarship: Awards Full tuition.

Eligibility: Applicant must be a graduate of De La Salle Middle School (St. Louis, Mo.) and/or one of the public or private high schools within the boundaries of Saint Louis City.

Requirements: Top Applicants.

Application Deadline: December 1

Application link:
https://www.maryville.edu/admissions/finan cial-aid/scholarships/

2 Fontbonne University

Location: St. Louis, Missouri
Setting: Suburban (16 Acres)
Undergraduate Enrollment: 665
Type: Private

Presidential Award: Awards Full tuition.

Eligibility: Applicants are notified by Invitation.

Requirements: Top Applicants.

Application Deadline: January 15

Application link:
https://www.fontbonne.edu/admission-aid/scholarships-tuition/scholarships-grants-loans/freshman-scholarships-institutional-aid/

3 Park University

Location: Parkville, Missouri
Setting: Suburban (700 Acres)
Undergraduate Enrollment: 8,504
Type: Private

McAfee Scholarship: Awards Full tuition.

Requirements: Two letters of recommendation from high school teachers | GPA 3.75+ | ACT 28/ SAT 1310 Recommended – Not Required | 300-500 word personal statement as described within application.

Application Deadline: November 1

Application link:
https://www.park.edu/academics/honors-academy/scholarships/

4 Culver-Stockton College

Location: Canton, Missouri
Setting: Rural (143 Acres)
Undergraduate Enrollment: 879
Type: Private

Pillars for Excellence: Awards Full tuition.

Requirements: A minimum cumulative high school GPA of 3.75 (4.0 scale) | 1230+ SAT/ 26+ ACT

Application Deadline: Check site for more details.

Application link:
https://culver.edu/admissions/scholarships-grants/

5 Columbia College

Location: Columbia, Missouri
Setting: Urban (231 Acres)
Undergraduate Enrollment: 7,861
Type: Private

Presidential Scholarship: Awards Full tuition.

Requirements: Top Applicants | A minimum 3.0 cumulative high school GPA.

Application Deadline: Check site for more details.

Application link:
https://www.ccis.edu/tuition-financial-aid/scholarships/traditional

6 University of Missouri, Columbia

Location: Columbia, Missouri
Setting: City (1,262 Acres)
Undergraduate Enrollment: 22,589
Type: Public

National Merit Finalist & Semifinalist Scholarship: Awards Full tuition and fees + $3,500 additional stipend + $10,964 one year on-campus housing and dining + one-time payments $2,000 for research/study abroad and a $1,000 for tech enrichment.

Eligibility: National Merit Finalist or Semifinalist | Awarded to *Missouri residents*.

Missouri Land Grant: Awards 100% of unmet need for tuition and fees.

Eligibility: Awarded to *Missouri residents* who are Pell-eligible students.

Application Deadline: November 15

Application link:
https://admissions.missouri.edu/scholarships/

7 Webster University

Location: Webster Groves, Missouri
Setting: Suburban (47 Acres)
Undergraduate Enrollment: 2,029
Type: Private

Chancellor's Scholarship: Awards Full tuition.

Requirements: A minimum 3.75 cumulative high school GPA (on a 4.0 scale) | A minimum 1260+ SAT | Rank in the top 20% of your high school graduating class.

Dr. Donald M. Suggs Scholarship: Awards Full tuition.

Requirements: A minimum 3.5 cumulative high school GPA (on a 4.0 scale) | A minimum ACT composite score of 25 or 1200+ SAT | Rank in the top 20% of your high school graduating class.

Check site for more details.

Application Deadline: January 18

Application link: https://www.webster.edu/financialaid/programs.php

8 University of Missouri – Kansas City

Location: Kansas City, Missouri
Setting: Urban (150 Acres)
Undergraduate Enrollment: 10,709
Type: Public

Henry W. Bloch Scholars: Awards Full tuition and fees.

Eligibility: Applicant must live in one of these five area counties – Clay, Jackson or Platte in Missouri, or Johnson or Wyandotte in Kansas | U.S. citizen or permanent resident | Demonstrate financial need – eligible or nearly eligible for the Pell Grant.

Marion H. Bloch Scholars: Awards Full tuition and fees.

Eligibility: Applicant must live in one of these five area counties – Clay, Jackson or Platte in Missouri, or Johnson or Wyandotte in Kansas | U.S. citizen or permanent resident

Requirements: A minimum ACT score of 29 or SAT equivalent | 3.6+ GPA.

Application Deadline: November 15

Application link: https://finaid.umkc.edu/financial-aid/scholarships/

9

Washington University in St. Louis

Location: St. Louis, Missouri
Setting: Urban (169 Acres)
Undergraduate Enrollment: 8,034
Type: Private

John B. Ervin Scholars Program: Awards Full tuition plus a $2,500 stipend.

Eligibility: Open to U.S. Citizens, permanent residents, and undocumented or DACA students living in the U.S.

Requirements: Top Applicants.

Annika Rodriguez Scholars Program: Awards Full tuition plus a $2,500 stipend.

Eligibility: Students who apply to any undergraduate division of Washington University may apply for the Annika Rodriguez Scholars Program.

College of Arts & Sciences

Arthur Holly Compton Fellowship Program: Awards Full tuition plus a $1,000 stipend.

McKelvey School of Engineering

Alexander S. Langsdorf Fellowships: Awards Full tuition plus a $1,000 stipend.

Sam Fox School of Design & Visual Arts

James W. Fitzgibbon Scholarships in Architecture: Awards Full tuition.

Requirements: Top Applicants.

Application Deadline: November 1

Application link: https://admissions.wustl.edu/cost-aid/scholarships/

10 Central Christian College Of The Bible

Location: Moberly, Missouri
Setting: City (40 Acres)
Undergraduate Enrollment: 300+
Type: Private

Full-Tuition Torch Scholarship: Awards Full tuition.

Requirements: Student must have a minimum of 3.5 high school GPA and a minium of 22 ACT (OR SAT Equivalent)

Application Deadline: January 1

Application link: http://cccb.edu/financial-aid/scholarships/full-tuition/

11 Rockhurst University

Location: Kansas City, Missouri
Setting: Urban (55 Acres)
Undergraduate Enrollment: 2,704
Type: Private

Trustees' Scholarship: Awards Full tuition.

Requirements: Top Applicants.

Check site for more details.

Application Deadline: January 1

Application link: https://www.rockhurst.edu/admissions/freshman/scholarships

1 Montana State University

Location: Bozeman, Montana
Setting: City (956 Acres)
Undergraduate Enrollment: 14,668
Type: Public

Presidential Scholarship: Full tuition waiver and a generous stipend renewable for up to four years.

P.S: Finalists who do not receive the Presidential Scholarship will be considered for the Provost Scholarship, which also provides a full tuition waiver and a stipend.

Requirements: Top Applicants.

Application Deadline: December 1

Application link:
https://www.montana.edu/admissions/scholarships/additional.html

2 University of Providence

Location: Great Falls, Montana
Setting: City (44 Arces)
Undergraduate Enrollment: 668
Type: Private

University of Providence Leadership Scholars: Award ranges from $18,000 to full tuition.

Requirements: A minimum 3.0 cumulative high school GPA.

University of Providence Catholic Scholars: Award ranges from $18,000 to full tuition.

Requirements: A minimum 3.0 cumulative high school GPA.

P.S: A separate application is required and includes an essay, resume, letter of recommendation from high school counselor, principal or teacher, and a campus interview.

Endowed Scholarships

Awards cover up to the cost of tuition.

Check site for more details.

Application Deadline: December 18

Application link:
https://www.uprovidence.edu/financial-services/scholarships/

1 Nebraska Wesleyan University

Location: Lincoln, Nebraska
Setting: City (50 Acres)
Undergraduate Enrollment: 1,706
Type: Private

TeamMates Access Scholarship:
Awards Full tuition.

Requirements: A minimum 3.0 cumulative high school GPA (on a 4.0 scale) | 25+ ACT, and be Federal Pell rant eligible as determined by a completed FAFSA (Free Application for Federal Student Aid) submitted to NWU.

Application Deadline: January 5

Application link:
https://www.nebrwesleyan.edu/admissions/financial-aid-office/undergraduate-aid/first-year-scholarships

2 Union College

Location: Lincoln, Nebraska
Setting: Suburban (50 Acres)
Undergraduate Enrollment: 579
Type: Private

Board of Trustees Scholarship: Awards Full tuition.

Requirements: A minimum 3.9 cumulative high school GPA | 33+ ACT (1500 SAT)

Application Deadline: February 15

Application link: https://ucollege.edu/financial

3

University of Nebraska at Kearney

Location: Kearney, Nebraska
Setting: City (501 Acres)
Undergraduate Enrollment: 4,427
Type: Public

In-State Scholarships

Board of Regents Scholarship: Awards Full tuition.

Requirements: Top Applicants.

Kearney Law Opportunities Program (KLOP): Awards Full tuition.

Requirements: A minimum 3.5 cumulative high school GPA | 27+ ACT

P.S: This scholarship is designed to recruit students from rural areas and train them to become **lawyers** who will return and practice in their communities.

Check site for full details on this scholarship.

Kearney Health Opportunities Program (KHOP): Awards Full tuition.

P.S: The purpose of the program is to recruit and educate students from rural Nebraska who are committed to returning to rural Nebraska to practice **healthcare**.

Requirements: Top Applicants.

Out-of-State Scholarships

Blue and Gold Scholarship: Awards Full tuition.

Requirements: Top Applicants.

Application Deadline: November 1

Application link: https://www.unk.edu/scholarships.php

4 University of Nebraska – Lincoln

Location: Lincoln, Nebraska
Setting: City (873 Acres)
Undergraduate Enrollment: 19,552
Type: Public

Chancellor's Tuition Scholarship: Awards Full tuition.

Eligibility: Awarded to finalists in nationally recognized scholar competitions, such as the National Merit and National Hispanic Recognition programs.

Regents Scholar Tuition Commitment: Awards Full tuition (**to in-state students**)

Requirements: Top Applicants.

Application Deadline: February 1

Application link:
https://admissions.unl.edu/cost/

5 Chadron State College

Location: Chadron, Nebraska
Setting: Rural (281 Acres)
Undergraduate Enrollment: 1,439
Type: Public

Gold Presidential Scholarship: Awards Full tuition.

Requirements: Top Applicants.

Application Deadline: January 15

Application link:
https://www.csc.edu/start/financial-aid/scholarships/

6 Creighton University

Location: Omaha, Nebraska
Setting: Urban (118 Acres)
Undergraduate Enrollment: 4,481
Type: Private

Markoe First Generation Scholarship: Awards Full tuition.

Requirements: A minimum 3.3 cumulative high school GPA (on a 4.0 scale) | Applicants must be defined as Federal Pell Grant eligible | Must be a first-generation student.

Application Deadline: January 15

Application link: https://www.creighton.edu/admission-aid/admissions-information/scholarships

7

Peru State College

Location: Peru, Nebraska
Setting: Rural (104 Acres)
Undergraduate Enrollment: 1,050
Type: Public

Board of Trustees Scholarship: Awards Full tuition.

Eligibility: Applicant must be a Nebraska high school graduate or resident.

Requirements: Top Applicants.

No Boundaries Scholarship: Awards Full tuition.

Eligibility: Applicant must be a **non-resident** of the state of Nebraska.

Requirements: Top Applicants.

Rural Health Opportunities Program (RHOP): Awards Full tuition.

Eligibility: Students admitted into the RHOP program must be from a rural background.

P.S: The purpose of the program is to recruit and educate students from rural communities who plan to return to rural areas to practice.

Application Deadline: December 1

Learn more: https://www.peru.edu/rhop/index.html

Application Deadline: January 15

Application link: https://www.peru.edu/affordability/competitive.html

Wayne State College

8

Location: Wayne, Nebraska
Setting: Rural (128 Acres)
Undergraduate Enrollment: 3,766
Type: Public

Neihardt Scholars Program: Full tuition, renewable double occupancy room waiver, and a $500 annual stipend for four years.

Requirements: A minimum 3.5 cumulative high school GPA (on a 4.0 scale) | 25+ ACT or an SAT score of at least 1200.

Presidential Scholarship: Awards Full tuition and half of the housing costs, renewable for 4 years.

Requirements: 30+ ACT or an SAT score of at least 1390.

NSCS Board of Trustees Scholarship: Awards Full tuition (**to Nebraska residents**)

Requirements: 25+ ACT or an SAT score of at least 1200.

Rural Health Opportunities Program (RHOP): Awards Full tuition.

Eligibility: Awarded to students from rural areas of Nebraska who demonstrate academic potential and a desire to practice medical laboratory science, dental hygiene, dentistry, medicine, nursing, pharmacy, physical therapy, physician assistant, or radiography in rural Nebraska.

Rural Law Opportunities Program (RLOP): Awards Full tuition (to students from rural areas of **Nebraska**)

Application Deadline: December 1

Application link: https://www.wsc.edu/scholarships

1 University of Nevada, Reno

Location: Reno, Nevada
Setting: City (200 Acres)
Undergraduate Enrollment: 17,025
Type: Public

Presidential Scholarship: Awards $8,000 per year. This covers the cost for *in-state tuition*.

Requirements: Have a minimum high school GPA of 3.5

National Merit Scholarship: Awards $16,000 per year. This covers *twice* the cost for *in-state tuition*.

Eligibility: Applicant must be a National Merit Finalist.

Application Deadline: February 1

Application link: https://www.unr.edu/financial-aid/scholarships

2 University of Nevada, Las Vegas

Location: Las Vegas, Nevada
Setting: Urban (358 Acres)
Undergraduate Enrollment: 25,407
Type: Public

University of Nevada, Las Vegas offers so many scholarship opportunities to incoming freshmen who wish to pursue an undergraduate degree in the instuition.

Check the website for an extensive list of scholarship opportunities:

https://www.unlv.edu/finaid/scholarships

1 University of New Hampshire

Location: Durham, New Hampshire

Setting: Suburban (2,600 Arces)

Undergraduate Enrollment: 11,490

Type: Public

Granite Guarantee: Awards Full tuition (***to in-state students***)

Eligibility: Applicants must be New Hampshire residents who are first-time, first-year, Pell Grant – eligible.

Check site for more details: https://admissions.unh.edu/granite-guarantee

Guard and Reserve Forces Duty Scholarships: Awards Full tuition and fees; monthly drill pay; monthly cadet stipend.

Application Deadline: November 15

Application link: https://www.unh.edu/financialaid/types-aid/scholarships

2 Southern New Hampshire University

Location: Manchester, New Hampshire

Setting: Suburban (338 Acres)

Undergraduate Enrollment: 2,777

Type: Private

Southern New Hampshire University Sets Out to Reimagine Campus-Based Learning, Offers ***Full Tuition*** Scholarships for Incoming Freshmen.

Check site for more details: https://www.snhu.edu/about-us/newsroom/press-releases/full-tuition-scholarships-for-incoming-freshmen

Southern New Hampshire University Scholarships: https://www.snhu.edu/tuition-and-financial-aid/paying-for-college/ways-to-save

1 New Jersey Institute of Technology

Location: Newark, New Jersey
Setting: Urban (48 Arces)
Undergraduate Enrollment: 9,183
Type: Public

National Merit Scholarship: Awards full tuition and fees to students who have been selected by the National Merit Scholarship Corporation (NMSC)

Requirements: To enter the competition, applicant must be either a U.S. citizen or a U.S. lawful permanent resident.

Honors Merit Awards: Awards up to full tuition and fees.

Requirements: Applicant must be accepted into the Albert Dorman Honors College to be eligible for this award.

Faculty Scholarships: Awards up to full tuition minus other tuition-based award.

Requirements: Top Applicants.

2 Saint Elizabeth University

Location: Morris Township, New Jersey
Setting: Suburban (200 Arces)
Undergraduate Enrollment: 752
Type: Private

Presidential Scholarship: Awards Full tuition to **in-state** residents.

Requirements: Top Applicants.

Application Deadline: March 1 (Fall Semester scholarships) | November 1 (Spring Semester scholarships)

Application link:
https://www.steu.edu/admissions/financial-aid/types-of-scholarships

Architecture Design Competition Scholarships: Awards Half to Full tuition.

P.S: This is a 5-year scholarship for freshmen majoring in Architecture.

Requirements: Applicant must be accepted into the New Jersey School of Architecture.

Application Deadline: September 30

Application link:
https://www.njit.edu/financialaid/merit-based-scholarships#njr

3 Caldwell University

Location: Caldwell, New Jersey
Setting: Suburban (70 Arces)
Undergraduate Enrollment: 1,630
Type: Private

Presidential Scholarship: Awards range from $20,000 to Full tuition.

Requirements: Awarded to top applicants with SAT scores exceeding 1270.

Application Deadline: December 1

Application link:
https://www.caldwell.edu/admissions/financial-aid/scholarships-and-grants/

4 Centenary University

Location: Hackettstown, New Jersey
Setting: Suburban (42 Arces)
Undergraduate Enrollment: 1,193
Type: Private

Hackettstown Partnership Scholarship: Awards Full tuition.

Eligibility: Awarded to a student who will be graduating from Hackettstown High School in the current school year.

Application link:
https://www.centenaryuniversity.edu/admission-aid/tuition-financial-aid/incoming-freshmen/

5 Stevens Institute of Technology

Location: Hoboken, New Jersey
Setting: City (55 Arces)
Undergraduate Enrollment: 3,932
Type: Private

The Ann P. Neupauer Scholarship: Awards Full tuition.

Requirements: Top Applicants.

Application Deadline: December 1

Application link: https://www.stevens.edu/admissions/tuition-financial-aid/undergraduate-scholarships-aid/stevens-scholarships

6 Fairleigh Dickinson University

Location: Teaneck, New Jersey
Setting: Suburban (266 Arces)
Undergraduate Enrollment: 7,860
Type: Private

Athletic Scholarships: Award varies up to Full tuition and housing.

P.S: Only available to *International students*.

Requirements: Recognizes superior athletic ability of students participating in the National Collegiate Athletic Association (NCAA) Division I | Only available at the Metropolitan Campus | Subject to Division I rules and regulations of the NCAA.

Learn more: https://www.fdu.edu/campuses/metropolitan-campus/campus-life/athletics/

Application Deadline: December 1

Application link: https://www.fdu.edu/admissions/international/scholarships/

7 The College of New Jersey

Location: Ewing, New Jersey
Setting: Suburban (289 Arces)
Undergraduate Enrollment: 6,959
Type: Public

Bonner Community Scholarship: Award value can cover from 50% to 100% of the cost of in-state tuition (financial need may be considered).

Requirements: Top Applicants.

Application Deadline: January 15

Application link: https://admissions.tcnj.edu/scholarships/instate scholarships/

8

Rutgers University

Location: New Brunswick, New Jersey
Setting: City (2,685 Arces)
Undergraduate Enrollment: 36,152
Type: Public

Rutgers University – New Brunswick

Scarlet Guarantee: Offers a "Last dollar" financial aid award that covers the cost of in-state tuition and mandatory fees.

Eligibility for the Scarlet Guarantee is based on your family's adjusted gross income (AGI) as reported on your FAFSA or NJAFAA and will be offered as part of your financial aid package.

Harvey Schwartz Scholarship: Awards full tuition.

Requirements: Top Applicants.

Rutgers University – Newark

TheDream.US : Awards up to $33,000 for high school graduate applicants obtaining a bachelor's degree. This covers the cost of Domestic tuition.

Application Deadline: February 28

This scholarship opportunity is for undocumented students and DREAMers!

Scholarships are awarded to help cover tuition, fees, books, supplies, and transportation expenses for students who would otherwise be unable to attend college.

Application Deadline: December 1

Application link: https://admissions.rutgers.edu/costs-and-aid/scholarships

Drew University

9

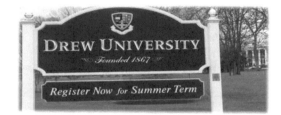

Location: Madison, New Jersey
Setting: Suburban (186 Arces)
Undergraduate Enrollment: 1,625
Type: Private

Army ROTC

Awards Full tuition, $1,200 book allowance per academic year and a monthly stipend.

Requirements: A minimum cumulative high school GPA of 2.50 | U.S. citizen between the ages of 17 and 26 | A minimum SAT score of 920 or 19 on the ACT. Please refer to this site for more details:

https://drew.edu/student-financial-services/sfs/financial-aid-scholarships/grants-scholarships/army-rotc/

Application Deadline: January 10

Application link: https://drew.edu/student-financial-services/sfs/financial-aid-scholarships/grants-scholarships/

Bloomfield College

10

Location: Bloomfield, New Jersey
Setting: Suburban (12 Arces)
Undergraduate Enrollment: 1,299
Type: Private

Bloomfield High School Scholarship: Awards Full tuition and books to **Bloomfield High School graduates.**

Requirements: A minimum 3.5 cumulative high school GPA (90) | SAT score of at least 1100 | Top five rank in class.

Trustees Scholar Awards: Awards range from $9,000 – Full tuition.

Requirements: A minimum 3.6 cumulative high school GPA (90) | 980+ SAT (Reading, Writing and Math sections) | College Prep Curriculum 4 + AP and/or Honor courses | Applicants must be U.S. citizens or permanent residents of the United States.

Presidential Scholar Awards: Awards range from $7,000 – Full tuition.

Requirements: A minimum 3.0 cumulative high school GPA (90) | 980+ SAT (Reading, Writing and Math sections) | College Prep Curriculum 2 + AP and/or Honor courses | Applicants must be U.S. citizens or permanent residents of the United States.

Application Deadline: October 1

Application link:
https://bloomfield.edu/courses/policy/scholarships-financial-aid

11 Seton Hall University

Location: South Orange, New Jersey
Setting: Suburban (58 Arces)
Undergraduate Enrollment: 6,063
Type: Private

ROTC Scholarships: Awards range from full tuition and fees or room and board.

Eligibility: Check site for more details.

Requirements: Top Applicants.

Application Deadline: January 15

Application link:
https://www.shu.edu/undergraduate-admissions/scholarships.cfm

12 Saint Peter's University

Location: Jersey City, New Jersey
Setting: Urban (25 Arces)
Undergraduate Enrollment: 2,134
Type: Private

Academic Award: Awards range from $9,000 to Full tuition.

Requirements: Top Applicants.

Application Deadline: March 15

Application link:
https://catalogs.saintpeters.edu/undergraduate/generalinformation/studentfinancialaid/

Kean University

13

Location: Union, New Jersey
Setting: Urban (240 Arces)
Undergraduate Enrollment: 10,573
Type: Public

Kean Scholar: Awards up to $20,000 per year. This covers the total cost of tuition.

Trustee Scholar: Awards up to $14,000. This covers the total cost of tuition for *in-state students*.

Requirements: Top Applicants.

New Jersey Center for Science, Technology and Mathematics (NJSTM) Scholarship: Awards 100% *in-state tuition* only.

Eligibility: Awarded to incoming freshmen who matriculate directly into five-year, combined bachelor/master's degree honors program.

Requirements: 3.7 – 4.0 HS GPA

Check site for more details.

Michael Graves College of Architecture and Design Scholarship: Awards Full *in-state tuition*.

Eligibility: Awarded to incoming freshmen who pursue undergraduate degrees in **Architecture or Design**.

Requirements: 3.0 unweighted HS GPA.

School of Fine and Performing Arts Scholarship: Awards Full *in-state tuition*.

Eligibility: Awarded to incoming freshmen who pursue undergraduate degrees in **Fine arts, Music or Theatre**.

Requirements: 3.0 unweighted HS GPA.

Kean Tuition Promise: Award may cover up to the full cost of tuition and fees.

Eligibility: Household adjusted gross income (AGI) is a maximum of $65k | Applicant must be a U.S. citizen or eligible noncitizen | Be a resident of New Jersey for at least one year before the first day of class.

Requirements: 3.2+ High school GPA.

Application Deadline: January 1

Application link:
https://www.kean.edu/offices/financial-aid/scholarship-services/merit-scholarships-new-incoming-students

1 University of New Mexico

Location: Albuquerque, New Mexico
Setting: Urban (769 Arces)
Undergraduate Enrollment: 15,336
Type: Public

Freshmen New Mexico Resident Scholarships:

Presidential Scholarship: Awards up to $10,000 per year. This covers the total cost of tuition.

Requirements: A minimum 3.75 cumulative high school GPA.

National African American Scholars: Awards up to $11,000 per year. This covers the total cost of tuition.

Eligibility: National African American Scholars.

National American Indian Scholars: Awards up to $11,000 per year. This covers the total cost of tuition.

Eligibility: National American Indian Scholars.

National Hispanic Scholars: Awards up to $11,000 per year. This covers the total cost of tuition.

Eligibility: National Hispanic Scholars.

2 New Mexico Institute of Mining & Technology

Location: Socorro, New Mexico
Setting: Rural (320 Arces)
Undergraduate Enrollment: 1,244
Type: Public

S-STEM Scholarship for New Freshman students Computer Science and Information Technology Majors: Awards up to $10,000 per year.

Requirements: High school GPA of at least 3.6 (from transcripts), or ranked in the top 15% of graduating high school class | U.S. citizen or permanent resident.

Application Deadline: May 31

Application link: https://www.nmt.edu/finaid/freshmen.php

Lobo First-Year Promise: Award covers 100% base tuition and fees.

Eligibility: Applicant must graduate from a New Mexico high school and have an annual family income of $50,000 or less.

Application Deadline: December 1

Application link: https://scholarship.unm.edu/

3   New Mexico State University

Location: Las Cruces, New Mexico
Setting: City (900 Arces)
Undergraduate Enrollment: 11,231
Type: Public

Conroy Honors Scholars: Award covers Full tuition and required fees. Recipients are eligible to receive a $2,500 Global Citizen Award to help fund a study abroad experience with guidance from the Honors College.

Requirements: 3.9 GPA or Academic Index of 159 and above.

Application Deadline: December 1

Application link: https://fa.nmsu.edu/scholarships/

4   New Mexico Highlands University

Location: Las Vegas, New Mexico
Setting: Rural (175 Arces)
Undergraduate Enrollment: 1,699
Type: Public

Regent's New Mexico Scholars Scholarship: Awards full tuition and fees plus $500 per semester.

Eligibility: Applicant must rank in the top 5 percent of graduating class or 25 ACT | Family income of $60,000 or less.

Application Deadline: March 1

Application link: https://www.nmhu.edu/financial-aid-2/scholarships/

Tuition-Free College for NEW MEXICANS:

New Mexico Higher Education Department has a provision for New Mexicans to attend College Tuition Free!

With the New Mexico Opportunity Scholarship, the New Mexico Lottery Scholarship, and more than 25 scholarships, grants, and college financial aid programs available, there are options for every New Mexican to pursue higher education without having to worry about the cost of tuition and fees.

Learn more: https://hed.nm.gov/free-college-for-new-mexico

1 Fordham University

Location: New York City, New York
Setting: Urban (125 Acres)
Undergraduate Enrollment: 9,904
Type: Private

Semifinalist and National Recognition Program Scholarships: Award covers Full tuition.

Requirements: Awarded to students who are designated as Semi-finalists by the National Merit Recognition Program or Scholars by the National Hispanic Recognition Program, African American Recognition Program, or Indigenous Recognition Program (new in 2021)

Excellence in Theatre Scholarship: Award covers Full tuition plus the average cost of a double room or actual charges, whichever is less (excluding meal plans and fees), if the recipient lives on campus. Requirements: Awarded to top theatre admits.

This Scholarships is available to out-of-state students and International students.

Fordham University **School of Law** has scholarships that covers up to the full cost of tuition.
Application Deadline: November 1

Application link:
https://www.fordham.edu/undergraduate-admission/apply/scholarships-and-grants/

2 Roberts Wesleyan College

Location: Rochester, New York
Setting: Suburban (188 Acres)
Undergraduate Enrollment: 1,111
Type: Private

B.T Roberts Scholarship: Awards Full tuition.

Requirements: Top Applicants.

P.S: This Scholarship will be awarded based on an interview during the event, an essay, and high school academic performance. Students must attend the **Academic Scholarship Celebration** to be eligible.

National Merit Scholarship: Awards Full tuition.

Eligibility: Awarded to National Merit Scholar Finalists.

Music Scholarship: Awards Full tuition.

Requirements: Awarded each year to the most skilled musicians who audition.

Application Deadline: February 14

Application link:
https://www.roberts.edu/undergraduate/tuition-and-aid/grants-scholarships/

3

Syracuse University

Location: Syracuse, New York
Setting: City (721 Arces)
Undergraduate Enrollment: 14,778
Type: Private

The 1870 Scholarship: Awards Full tuition.

P.S: Prospective recipients are evaluated for academic and creative accomplishments, commitment in community service and demonstrated financial need. The award is offered to students in all colleges.

Coronat Scholars Program: Awards Full tuition plus other benefits.

Requirements: A mean high school GPA of 4.15 | A mean SAT score of 1480 (combined math and verbal)

Junior Achievement Scholarship: Award covers Full tuition.

P.S: This Scholarship is awarded by Syracuse University to outstanding first-year student who has applied **through Junior Achievement of CNY**. Selection is made jointly by Junior Achievement of CNY and Syracuse University based on academic record, quality of work in JA, personal achievement, and an interview.

Application Deadline: November 15

Application link: https://financialaid.syr.edu/scholarships/su/

NFTE Scholarship: Awards Full tuition and mandatory fees.

Requirements: Students must file for financial aid and submit both the CSS/Financial Aid PROFILE and FAFSA to be considered | Students must be a U.S. citizen or a permanent resident.

P.S: The Office of Financial Aid and Scholarship Programs will identify scholars who are both alumni of the NFTE program and admitted under regular Syracuse University Office of Admissions guidelines.

Refugee Scholarship: Award covers Full tuition and fees.

P.S: This program is administered by the Office of Admissions with the Office of Financial Aid and Scholarship Programs. Students should follow normal admissions and financial aid deadlines.

Say Yes to Education: Award covers Full tuition, fees and books.

Requirements: Applicants must file for financial aid and submit both the CSS/Financial Aid PROFILE and FAFSA to be considered. Check site for more details.

4 Oswego State University of New York

Location: Oswego, New York
Setting: Rural (700 Acres)
Undergraduate Enrollment: 6,673
Type: Public

Excelsior Scholarship Program: Awards Full tuition.

Eligibility: New York residents.

Through New York State's Excelsior Scholarship program, a greater number of **New York students and families** will be eligible to earn free tuition at SUNY Oswego.

Check site for more details.

"Free Tuition Plus" Scholarships: Awards Full tuition.

Eligibility: New York residents.

Check site for more details.

Application Deadline: November 15 (for spring term applicants) | January 15 (for fall term applicants)

Application link: https://www.oswego.edu/financial-aid/scholarships

5 D'youville College

Location: Buffalo, New York
Setting: Urban (17 Acres)
Undergraduate Enrollment: 1,388
Type: Private

Dillon Scholarship: Awards Full tuition.

Diocese of Buffalo Catholic High School Scholarship: Awards Full tuition.

Requirements: Top Applicants.

SAY YES: Awards Full tuition.

D'Youville offers unlimited Say Yes Full-Tuition Scholarships to high school students who graduate from a Say Yes eligible schools.

Requirements: In order to be considered for the Say Yes tuition scholarship, the annual family income cannot exceed $75,000. Family income is determined by the FAFSA and D'Youville's financial aid office.

Check site for more details.

Application Deadline: February 1

Application link: http://www.dyc.edu/admissions/financial-aid-scholarships/types-of-aid/scholarships/undergraduate.aspx

6 University of Rochester

Location: Rochester, New York
Setting: Urban (707 Acres)
Undergraduate Enrollment: 6,570
Type: Private

International Baccalaureate (IB) Scholarship: Awards Full tuition.

Eligibility: Awarded to students who successfully complete **the International Baccalaureate diploma at Wilson Magnet High School**.

Regents Scholar Tuition Commitment: Awards Full tuition.

Requirements: Top Applicants.

SAY YES TO EDUCATION: Awards Full tuition.

P.S: Say Yes students who are admitted to the College, including all qualified graduates of the Syracuse and Buffalo City School Districts, and **whose family income is less than or equal to $100,000, will receive full tuition funding** through a combination of federal, state and university grants.

Application Deadline: November 1

Application link:
https://www.rochester.edu/financial-aid/scholarships/

7 Elmira College

Location: Elmira, New York
Setting: City (55 Acres)
Undergraduate Enrollment: 632
Type: Private

Elmira Scholars Program: Awards Full tuition.

Requirements: A 3.9 GPA (No SAT or ACT scores required) | A 3.7 GPA as well as 1300 SAT or 28 ACT composite score.

Check out the Phi Theta Kappa Scholarship.

As a Phi Theta Kappa Scholar, you will receive **a one-term, full-tuition scholarship** to determine if you would like to earn your four-year degree at a nationally-ranked, private college.

ROTC Scholarships

Scholarship for High School Students: Awards Full tuition, $1200 per year in book money, mandatory fees, and a monthly stipend that increases each academic year.

Requirements: Top Applicants.

Application Deadline: December 12

Application link:
https://www.elmira.edu/affordability/undergraduate-tuition-aid/scholarships/scholarships

8 St. Lawrence University

Location: Canton, New York
Setting: Rural (1,100 Acres)
Undergraduate Enrollment: 2,247
Type: Private

Trustee Scholarship: Awards Full tuition.

Requirements: Top Applicants.

This scholarship is awarded to the top first-year students.
Based on academic excellence, character, and leadership.

Kirk Douglas Scholarship: Awards Full tuition and fees.

Eligibility: By Invitation only, the Kirk Douglas Scholarship is for students from under-represented and low-income backgrounds who show ambition and potential to contribute to diversity within the campus community.

Application Deadline: January 1

Application link:
https://www.stlawu.edu/offices/admissions-office/scholarships

9 Clarkson University

Location: Potsdam, New York
Setting: Rural (640 Acres)
Undergraduate Enrollment: 2,852
Type: Private

Clarkson Ignite Presidential Fellows Program: Award covers Full tuition.

Requirements: Top Applicants.

Application Deadline: January 15

Application link:
https://www.clarkson.edu/undergraduate-admissions/1st-year-students-financial-aid-costs-scholarships

10 Hofstra University

Location: Hempstead, New York

Setting: Suburban (244 Acres)

Undergraduate Enrollment: 6,050

Type: Private

Hofstra University Trustee Scholars Program: Awards Full tuition.

Requirements: An average SAT/ACT equivalent of 1530 on a 1600 scale | Weighted GPA of 4.24 | Top 10% of HS graduating class.

Check out the **Provost Academic Excellence Scholarship** offered by Hofstra University to graduates of Nassau Community College.

Learn more: https://www.hofstra.edu/admission/adm_scholarship_provostncc.html

Application Deadline: November 15

Application link: https://www.hofstra.edu/admission/first-year-scholarships.html

11 SUNY Polytechnic Institute

Location: Albany, New York

Setting: Suburban (800 Acres)

Undergraduate Enrollment: 2,043

Type: Public

Excelsior Scholarship Program: Award when combined with other grants/scholarships, allows students who are **New York State residents**, and whose families earn $125,000 or less annually to attend SUNY Polytechnic Institute **tuition free!**

Application Deadline: December 1

Application link: https://sunypoly.edu/admissions/undergraduate/first-year-information/scholarships.html

12 Molloy College

Location: Rockville Centre, New York
Setting: Suburban (30 Acres)
Undergraduate Enrollment: 3,308
Type: Private

Molloy College Scholar's Program: Awards Full tuition.

Requirements: Applicants must have a minimum of 95% High school average | A minimum score of 1380 on the SAT combined from critical reading and math or a minimum of 30 on the ACT.

Athletic Grants: Grants up to Full tuition.

P.S: Awarded to full-time students based on athletic ability.

Fine Arts and Performing Arts Scholarships: Awards up to Full tuition.

Eligibility: Awarded to entering full-time freshmen who are judged to have exceptional talent or have achieved proficiency in art, music or communication arts. Qualifications are demonstrated through audition, the submission of a portfolio or other documented experience.

Application Deadline: December 15

Application link:
https://www.molloy.edu/admissions/financial-aid/scholarships/freshmen-and-transfer-students

13 Lehman College, CUNY

Location: The Bronx borough, New York
Setting: Urban (37 Acres)
Undergraduate Enrollment: 12,375
Type: Public

Excelsior Scholarship Program: Award when combined with other grants/scholarships, allows eligible full-time students to attend Lehman College, *tuition free!*

Eligibility: New York residents.

Application Deadline: December 1

Application link:
https://www.lehman.edu/financial-aid/scholarships.php

14 College of Mount Saint Vincent

Location: New York City, New York
Setting: Urban (70 Acres)
Undergraduate Enrollment: 2,281
Type: Private

Premier Programs

Corazon C. Aquino Scholarship: Awards Full tuition.

Eligibility: Awarded to high achieving incoming first-year students of Filipino descent.

P.S: Applicants will be required to complete an interview with the Aquino Scholarship Committee as a part of their application for this scholarship.

There are Full room and board Scholarships also available under the Premier Programs.

Application Deadline: February 15

Application link:
https://mountsaintvincent.edu/admission/fin
ancial-aid/financial-aid-
options/scholarships/premier-programs/

15 New York University

Location: New York City, New York
Setting: Urban (230 Acres)
Undergraduate Enrollment: 28,772
Type: Private

AnBryce Scholarships: Awards Full tuition.

Eligibility: Awarded to students who demonstrate financial need and who are the first generation in their family to attend college. Please refer to this site for more details: https://www.nyu.edu/admissions/undergraduate-admissions/aid-and-costs/scholarships.html#incoming

NYU Wagner Merit Scholarships

Dean's Scholarship: Awards Full tuition.

Requirements: Top Applicants.

Nneka Fritz (WAG '08) Scholarship: Awards up to Full tuition.

Eligibility: Awarded to students from historically underrepresented groups with an interest in economic development.

P.S: Candidates should ideally be committed to using their education to benefit the Newark Area of New Jersey.

Application Deadline: February 20

Application link:
https://wagner.nyu.edu/admissions/financial-aid/scholarships

16

CUNY Bernard M Baruch College

Location: New York City, New York
Setting: Urban (3 Arces)
Undergraduate Enrollment: 15,774
Type: Public

Clark Foundation Student Scholarship: Awards Full and partial tuition scholarships.

Eligibility: Awarded to students in the Marxe School of Public and International Affairs.

P.S: Recipients will be chosen on a merit basis.

Dora and Hyman Rosenzweig Scholarship: Awards Full tuition.

Eligibility: Awarded to incoming freshmen who demonstrate financial need and plan to pursue a major in the *Zicklin School of Business.*

Karl and Helen Meyer Scholarship: Award covers Full tuition.

Eligibility: Awarded to an incoming freshman who is a first generation American or an immigrant and who demonstrates financial need and academic promise.

Lubov and Elizavet Geiman Scholarship: Awards Full tuition.

Eligibility: Awarded to an incoming freshman who is a first generation American or an immigrant, demonstrates significant financial need and plans to study in the *Zicklin School of Business*.

P.S: Preference is for students who worked during high school.

Max Brenner Scholarship: Awards Full tuition.

Eligibility: Awarded to applicants who plan to pursue a major in Accounting.

Sarah and Sol Laterman Scholarship: Awards annual Full and partial tuition scholarships.

Eligibility: Awarded to incoming freshmen who are *graduates of Stuyvesant High School*, currently located at 345 Chambers Street, New York, NY, or its successors in interest, who have outstanding academic credentials.

Application Deadline: December 1

Application link:
https://baruch.scholarships.ngwebsolutions.com/CMXAdmin/Cmx_Content.aspx?cpId=1119

17 Ithaca College

Location: Ithaca, New York
Setting: Suburban (670 Acres)
Undergraduate Enrollment: 4,818
Type: Private

Ithaca Opportunity Grant (IOG): Awards up to the Full cost of tuition.

Eligibility: Applicants must be of African American, Asian/Pacific Island, Hispanic, or Native American origin | Have considerable financial need.

Application Deadline: February 1

Application link:
https://www.ithaca.edu/tuition-financial-aid/financial-aid-basics/grants/ithaca-grants

18 CUNY John Jay College of Criminal Justice

Location: New York City, New York
Setting: Urban
Undergraduate Enrollment: 13,146
Type: Public

Excelsior Scholarship: Awards Full tuition.

Requirements: Applicants should file the FAFSA and the NYS Tuition Assistance Program (TAP) application | Have a family income of $125,000 or less

Application Deadline: February 1

Application link:
https://www.jjay.cuny.edu/excelsior-scholarship

19 Hobart and William Smith Colleges

Location: Geneva, New York
Setting: City (170 Acres)
Undergraduate Enrollment: 1,660
Type: Private

Seneca Scholarship: Awards Full tuition.

Requirements: Top Applicants.

P.S: In order to be considered for any scholarship(s), applicants must indicate interest by selecting "yes" to merit scholarship interest in your Common Application questions.

Check site for more details.

Application Deadline: February 1

Application link:
https://www2.hws.edu/admissions/merit-based-awards/

20 Morrisville State College

Location: Morrisville, New York
Setting: Rural (150 Acres)
Undergraduate Enrollment: 1,957
Type: Public

Excelsior Scholarship: Awards up to Full tuition.

P.S: This is a program designed to provide tuition-free college at New York's public colleges and universities to families making up to $125,000 a year.

Eligibility: New York resident | Family household adjusted gross income must not exceed $125,000 | Good academic standing.

Application Deadline: January 15

Application link:
https://www.morrisville.edu/contact/office s/financial-aid/excelsior-scholarship

21 SUNY College at Geneseo

Location: Geneseo, New York
Setting: Rural (220 Acres)
Undergraduate Enrollment: 4,295
Type: Public

NYS Excelsior Scholarship: Awards up to Full tuition.

Eligibility: New York resident | Family household adjusted gross income must not exceed $125,000 | Good academic standing.

Application Deadline: January 15

Application link:
https://www.geneseo.edu/financial_aid/private-state-scholarships

22 Alfred State College of Technology

Location: Alfred, New York
Setting: Rural (1,062 Acres)
Undergraduate Enrollment: 3,667
Type: Public

NYS Science, Technology, Engineering and Mathematics (STEM) Incentive Program: Awards up to Full tuition.

P.S: This program provides a full SUNY or CUNY tuition scholarship for the top 10 percent of students in each New York State high school if they pursue a STEM degree in an associate or bachelor degree program and agree to work in a STEM field in New York State for 5 years after graduation.

Eligibility: Applicant must be a New York resident | Be a U.S. citizen or eligible non-citizen | Be ranked in the top 10% of their high school graduating class of a NYS high school.

Excelsior Scholarship: Awards up to Full tuition.

Eligibility: New York resident | Family household adjusted gross income must not exceed $125,000 | Good academic standing.

Application Deadline: May 15

Application link: https://www.alfredstate.edu/financial-aid/scholarships/new-york-state-scholarships

23 University at Buffalo

Location: Buffalo, New York
Setting: Suburban (1,350 Acres)
Undergraduate Enrollment: 21,467
Type: Public

Walter E. Schmid Family Foundation Scholarship: Awards up to Full tuition and fees.

Requirements: Applicant must be an incoming first year student from Western New York (WNY) pursuing a degree in the **School of Engineering and Applied Sciences** who has demonstrated high academic achievement in high school and entrepreneurial interests.

Presidential Scholarship: Awards $15,000 Annually. (This covers the total cost of tuition for **in-state students**)

Requirements: Top Applicants.

Application Deadline: December 15

Application link: https://admissions.buffalo.edu/costs/scholarships.php

24

Vaughn College of Aeronautics and Technology

Location: New York City, New York
Setting: Urban (6 Acres)
Undergraduate Enrollment: 1,284
Type: Private

A "Futureproof" Tuition-Free Education Scholarship Program: Awards Full tuition.

Eligibility: Applicants must reside in Queens County, NY.

Requirements: A minimum cumulative grade point average (GPA) of at least an 80% | Minimum cumulative score of 1,000 on the SAT or 22 on the ACT | Applicant must submit academic accomplishments, intellectual and creative distinctions, extracurricular activities, letters of reference and original essays.

Application Deadline: March 1

Application link: https://www.vaughn.edu/blog/a-futureproof-tuition-free-education-could-be-yours-with-the-port-authority-scholarship/

1 Gardner Webb University

Location: Boiling Springs, North Carolina

Setting: Rural (240 Acres)

Undergraduate Enrollment: 1,977

Type: Private

Ignite Excellence Full Tuition Scholarships: Awards Full tuition.

Requirements: Top Applicants.

Application Deadline: January 15

Application link: https://gardner-webb.edu/admissions-aid/scholarships-and-grants/

2 Elizabeth City State University

Location: Elizabeth City, North Carolina

Setting: Rural (154 Acres)

Undergraduate Enrollment: 1,956

Type: Public

The Jackie Robinson Foundation: Awards $6,000 per year (This covers the total cost of tuition and fees for **in-state students**)

Requirements: Top Applicants.

Application Deadline: January 15

Application link: https://www.ecsu.edu/veterans/Scholarships.html

3 Lees-McRae College

Location: Banner Elk, North Carolina

Setting: Rural (460 Acres)

Undergraduate Enrollment: 872

Type: Private

Elizabeth McRae Scholarship: Awards Full tuition.

P.S: Recipients are chosen from all students invited to attend Scholars Day-An event in the spring that includes an interview and essay competition.

Requirements: Top Applicants.

Application Deadline: December 15

Application link: https://www.lmc.edu/admissions/financial-aid/types-of-aid.htm

4 Montreat College

Location: Montreat, North Carolina
Setting: Suburban (89 Acres)
Undergraduate Enrollment: 830
Type: Private

Honors Scholarship: Awards Full tuition.

Requirements: A minimum 3.5 unweighted high school GPA | A minimum qualifying test score of 1200 SAT, 25 ACT, or 78 CLT.

Application Deadline: January 14

Application link:
https://www.montreat.edu/admissions/tuition-aid/undergraduate/scholarships/

5 Meredith College

Location: Raleigh, North Carolina
Setting: Urban (225 Acres)
Undergraduate Enrollment: 1,427
Type: Private

Meredith presidential Scholarship:
Awards Full tuition and an opportunity for study abroad experience.

Requirements: A minimum unweighted high school GPA of 3.8 (4.0 grading scale) – 4.3 (weighted) | Superior standardized test scores SAT/ACT - 1480/33

Application Deadline: January 15

Application link:
https://www.meredith.edu/financial-assistance/financial-assistance-undergraduate-scholarships/

6 University of North Carolina – Wilmington

Location: Wilmington, North Carolina
Setting: Urban (661 Acres)
Undergraduate Enrollment: 14,488
Type: Public

SOAR Ambassador Program: Award covers *in-state* tuition and fees. A supplemental $1,000 award is added during the sophomore, junior and senior years.

Requirements: Top Applicants.

Honors Merit Scholarship: Awards may range from $500 a year to an award equivalent of in-state tuition and fees (~$7,500 per year).

Application Deadline: March 1

Application link:
https://uncw.edu/finaid/scholarships.html

7
University of North Carolina, Charlotte

Location: Charlotte, North Carolina

Setting: Urban (1,000 Acres)

Undergraduate Enrollment: 24,116

Type: Public

Levine Scholars Program: Awards 105,000 four year in-state tuition | 155,000 four year out-of-state tuition.

Requirements: Top Applicants.

Learn more about becoming a Future Levine Scholar here: https://levinescholars.charlotte.edu/

Belk Scholars program in Business Analytics: Award covers *In-state* tuition and fees.

Requirements: Unweighted high school GPA of 3.50-4.00 or a weighted high school GPA of 3.75-4.00.

Freeman Endowed Scholarships: Award covers *In-state* tuition and fees.

Requirements: Unweighted high school GPA of 3.20-4.00.

Johnson Scholarship: Award covers *In-state* tuition and fees.

Requirements: Unweighted high school GPA of 3.20-4.00.

Application Deadline: December 15

Application link: https://ninercentral.charlotte.edu/financial-aid-loans/types-aid/scholarships

8
North Carolina Wesleyan University

Location: Rocky Mount, North Carolina

Setting: Suburban (200 Acres)

Undergraduate Enrollment: 1,375

Type: Private

Trustee Scholarship: Awards Full tuition and books.

Requirements: A minimum 3.75 weighted GPA | 1200 SAT/ 25 ACT scores.

Application Deadline: December 1

Application link: https://ncwc.edu/scholarships/

9 Appalachian State University

Location: Boone, North Carolina
Setting: Rural (500 Acres)
Undergraduate Enrollment: 18,555
Type: Public

Signature Scholarships

Dr Willie C. Fleming Scholarship: Award covers Full *In-state* tuition and fees plus other benefits.

Requirements: Top Applicants.

Diversity Scholars Program Scholarship: Award covers Full *In-state* tuition and fees plus other benefits.

Requirements: Top Applicants.

Application Deadline: November 15

Application link: https://scholarships.appstate.edu/signature-scholarships

10 Warren Wilson College

Location: Swannanoa, North Carolina
Setting: Suburban (1,135 Acres)
Undergraduate Enrollment: 625
Type: Private

Milepost One: Awards Full tuition.

Requirements: A minimum 3.0 weighted GPA | Have a Total Family Income equal or less than $125,000.

Application Deadline: February 1

Application link: https://www.warren-wilson.edu/admission/tuition-and-aid/scholarships/

11 East Carolina University

Location: Greenville, North Carolina
Setting: City (1,600 Acres)
Undergraduate Enrollment: 22,463
Type: Public

Chancellor's Fellows: Award covers *In-state* tuition.

Requirements: Top Applicants.

The Department of Engineering PIRATES Scholars Program: Awards up to $10,000. (This covers the total cost of tuition and fees for **in-state students**)

Eligibility: This scholarship will be awarded to high-achieving incoming freshmen in the Department of Engineering with demonstrated financial need.

Requirements: An unweighted high school GPA of 3.0 or better and must intend to earn a B.S. in Engineering from the Department of Engineering at ECU.

Please refer to this site for more details: https://math.ecu.edu/scholarships/

Application Deadline: October 1

Application link: https://news.ecu.edu/2020/12/08/ecu-scholarships-guide/

12 Queens University of Charlotte

Location: Charlotte, North Carolina
Setting: Urban (95 Acres)
Undergraduate Enrollment: 1,440
Type: Private

Presidential Scholarship: Awards Full tuition.

Requirements: Top Applicants.

Application Deadline: February 1

Application link: https://www.queens.edu/admissions-aid/tuition-scholarship-aid/freshman-transfer-scholarships/

13 Catawba College

Location: Salisbury, North Carolina
Setting: Suburban (276 Acres)
Undergraduate Enrollment: 1,143
Type: Private

Socratic Scholarship: Awards Full tuition.

Requirements: Applicants must have a weighted GPA of 4.0+ or an unweighted GPA of 3.5+

The Spirit of Catawba Scholarship: Awards Full tuition.

Requirements: Top Applicants.

Application Deadline: November 1

Application link: https://catawba.edu/scholarships/

14 Salem College

Location: Winston-Salem, North Carolina
Setting: City (57 Acres)
Undergraduate Enrollment: 367
Type: Private

Outstanding applicants may receive four years of full tuition or full cost of attendance (tuition, fees, room, and board) through named awards such as the **Chatham, Elberson, Kick, Womble, and Whitaker, Davis Art** scholarships.

Check site for more details…

Scholarships for the FLEER Center

Pat Etheridge Scholarship: Awards Full tuition.

Eligibility: This scholarship is awarded to a full time Fleer student taking up to 24 semester hour who has declared their major of either Religion, Philosophy, History, or English with the preference being Religion.

Learn more: https://www.salem.edu/adult-students/scholarships

Requirements: Top Applicants.

Application Deadline: November 1

Application link: https://www.salem.edu/admissions/scholarships

Davidson College

Location: Davidson, North Carolina
Setting: Suburban (665 Acres)
Undergraduate Enrollment: 1,973
Type: Private

Nomination Scholarships

Lowell L. Bryan Scholarship: Award covers Full tuition and fees.

Eligibility: This scholarship is awarded to students who will contribute in a superlative manner to their sports as well as to academic and co-curricular life at Davidson.

Competition Scholarships

William Holt Terry Scholarship: Award covers Full tuition and fees, and a $3,000 special opportunity stipend.

Eligibility: Applicants should demonstrate exemplary leadership skills and personal qualities through student government, athletics, service, or other activities.

Application Scholarships

James B. Duke Scholarship: Award covers Full tuition and fees plus a $5,000 stipend.

Requirements: Top Applicants.

Application Deadline: November 15

Application link: https://www.davidson.edu/admission-and-financial-aid/financial-aid/scholarships

University of North Dakota

Location: Grand Forks, North Dakota
Setting: City (521 Acres)
Undergraduate Enrollment: 9,718
Type: Public

National Merit Scholars

This scholarship is awarded to National Merit Scholar Finalist or Semi-Finalist from North Dakota or Minnesota.

Awards Full tuition and mandatory student fees.

Requirements: National Merit Finalist/Semi-Finalist | Applicant must select UND as first choice on the National merit application.

Hudson & Christine Washburn Scholarship: Awards up to $12,000. (This covers the total cost of tuition and fees for *in-state students*)

Eligibility: This scholarship will be awarded to incoming freshmen students who are from *LaMoure County*.

Requirements: A minimum High school GPA of 3.0

Application Deadline: December 15

Application link: https://und.edu/one-stop/financial-aid/scholarships.html

2 University of Jamestown

Location: Jamestown, North Dakota
Setting: Rural (110 Arces)
Undergraduate Enrollment: 1,018
Type: Private

Wilson Scholarship: Awards Full tuition.

Requirements: A minimum 3.5 High School GPA (on a 4.0 scale) | An ACT composite score of 24 or SAT of 1160 | Candidates participate in on-campus interviews.

P.S: This scholarship is by invitation only.

ND Scholars Program: Awards Full tuition scholarships to qualifying **North Dakota high school graduates** who choose to stay in North Dakota to earn a first bachelor's degree.

Requirements: Applicants should score at or above the ninety-fifth percentile among those who took the ACT or SAT prior to July 1st of the calendar year preceding the individual's enrollment in college.

Application Deadline: October 15

Application link:
https://www.uj.edu/admission-aid/financial-aid-scholarships/scholarships/

3 Mayville State University

Location: Mayville, North Dakota
Setting: Rural (55 Arces)
Undergraduate Enrollment: 1,147
Type: Public

ND Scholars Program: Awards Full tuition scholarships to qualifying **North Dakota high school graduates** who choose to stay in North Dakota to earn a first bachelor's degree.

Requirements: Applicants should score at or above the ninety-fifth percentile among those who took the ACT or SAT prior to July 1st of the calendar year preceding the individual's enrollment in college.

Application Deadline: July 1

Application link: https://mayvillestate.edu/paying-school/scholarships/

1 University of Cincinnati

Location: Cincinnati, Ohio
Setting: Urban (253 Acres)
Undergraduate Enrollment: 28,910
Type: Public

Darwin T. Turner Scholarship Program: Award covers in-state tuition, fees, and book stipend per semester for four years.

Requirements: A minimum cumulative high school GPA of 3.0 (based on an unweighted 4.0 scale) | A minimum 24 composite ACT or 1160 combined SAT-R.

NEXT Innovation Scholars Program: Awards Full tuition and some supplemental educational expenses.

Requirements: Top Applicants.

Application Deadline: December 1

Application link: https://www.uc.edu/about/financial-aid/aid/scholarships.html

2 Ohio State University

Location: Columbus, Ohio
Setting: Urban (1,665 Acres)
Undergraduate Enrollment: 47,106
Type: Public

Morrill Scholarship Program

Awards Levels:

Prominence (the value of in-state tuition plus the non-resident surcharge for non-residents)

Excellence (the value of in-state tuition for Ohio residents).

Criteria: The Morrill Scholarship is awarded on a competitive basis to students admitted to the Columbus campus for the autumn semester following high school graduation. Applicants must be U.S. citizens or legal permanent residents of the United States.

Requirements: Top Applicants.

Application Deadline: December 1

Application link: http://undergrad.osu.edu/cost-and-aid/merit-based-scholarships

3 Ohio Northern University

Location: Ada, Ohio
Setting: Rural (342 Acres)
Undergraduate Enrollment: 2,426
Type: Private

Mathile Scholarship: Awards Full tuition.

Requirements: A minimum ACT score of 30 (1360 SAT, evidence-based reading and writing plus math) | A minimum high school GPA of 3.50.

James F. Dicke Scholarship: Awards Full tuition.

Requirements: A minimum ACT score of 29 (1330 SAT, evidence-based reading and writing plus math) | A minimum high school GPA of 3.50.

Application Deadline: December 1

Application link:
https://www.onu.edu/admissions-aid/financial-aid/undergraduate-scholarships

4 Cedarville University

Location: Cedarville, Ohio
Setting: Rural (850 Acres)
Undergraduate Enrollment: 4,191
Type: Private

Foster Care and Adoption Scholarship: Awards Full tuition.

Eligibility: Awarded to a student who has grown up in the foster care system and is now seeking to enroll at Cedarville.

Application Deadline: March 15

Application link:
https://www.cedarville.edu/cf/finaid/scholarships/currentaid/

5 Wittenberg University

Location: Springfield, Ohio
Setting: City (114 Acres)
Undergraduate Enrollment: 1,286
Type: Private

Bill Martin Scholarship: Awards Full tuition.

Requirements: Top Applicants.

P.S: Applicants of the Bill Martin Scholarship must reside in Washtenaw, Houghton or Keweenaw County, Michigan.

Application Deadline: December 1

Application link:
https://www.wittenberg.edu/admission/scholarship-opportunities

6 Xavier University

Location: Cincinnati, Ohio
Setting: Urban (175 Arces)
Undergraduate Enrollment: 5,145
Type: Private

ROTC Scholarships

Army ROTC: Award covers full tuition and educational fees, a $1,200 yearly book allowance and a monthly stipend starting at $300/month during the academic school year.

Requirements: Top Applicants.

Application Deadline: December 1

Application link:
https://www.xavier.edu/undergraduate-admission/tuition-and-aid/index

7 Case Western Reserve University

Location: Cleveland, Ohio
Setting: Urban (267 Arces)
Undergraduate Enrollment: 5,792
Type: Private

Andrew and Eleanor Squire Scholarship: Awards Full tuition.

P.S: Open to first-year applicants in the arts; humanities; management; accountancy; and natural, social and behavioral sciences.

Louis Stokes Congressional Black Caucus Foundation Scholarship: Awards Full tuition plus a grant of up to $2,500 for computer and book purchases, and assistance securing a paid summer internship.

Alexander A. Treuhaft Memorial Scholarship: Awards Full tuition.

P.S: Open to first-year applicants in Science and Engineering.

Performing Arts Scholarships: Awards Full tuition (to students who exhibit excellence in the **performing arts**.)

Requirements: Top Applicants.

Application Deadline: January 15

Application link: https://case.edu/admission/tuition-aid/scholarships

8 Marietta College

Location: Marietta, Ohio
Setting: Suburban (90 Arces)
Undergraduate Enrollment: 1,173
Type: Private

Trustee Scholarship: Awards Full tuition.

Rickey Physics Scholarship: Awards Full tuition.

Please refer to this site for more details: https://www.marietta.edu/physics-scholarships

Requirements: Top Applicants.

Charles Summer Harrison: Awards Full tuition.

P.S: Applicants are invited to submit a one-page statement on how they have impacted or promoted social justice and inclusion in their community.

Application Deadline: February 15

Application link: https://www.marietta.edu/scholarships

9 Cleveland State University

Location: Cleveland, Ohio
Setting: Urban (85 Acres)
Undergraduate Enrollment: 10,626
Type: Public

Honors Program: Awards Full in-state tuition for up to eight semesters.

Requirements: A minimum of 30 ACT composite score or 1380 SAT score | Applicant should rank in the top 10% of their high school class.

Ruth Ann Moyer Scholarship: Awards Full in-state tuition.

Eligibility: Applicants must be an Ohio resident, non-traditional (at least twenty-five years of age) student, has accepted admission and submitted final transcripts by June 15.

P.S: To apply for this scholarship, you must submit a brief personal essay describing yourself, including your future plans, any challenges you may have faced and overcome, and what receiving this scholarship means to you.

Application Deadline: January 15

Application link:
https://www.csuohio.edu/financial-aid/new-incoming-freshman

10 Baldwin Wallace University

Location: Berea, Ohio
Setting: Suburban (100 Acres)
Undergraduate Enrollment: 2,829
Type: Private

Say Yes Scholarship: Awards up to the Full cost of tuition.

Eligibility: Awarded to students attending eligible schools within the Cleveland Metropolitan School District.

Application Deadline: May 15

Application link:
https://www.bw.edu/undergraduate-admission/first-year/tuition/

11 Capital University

Location: Bexley, Ohio
Setting: Urban (48 Acres)
Undergraduate Enrollment: 2,090
Type: Private

Collegiate Fellowship: Awards Full tuition.

Requirements: A minimum high school GPA of 3.75 (on a 4.0 scale)

Capital Scholars Award: Awards Full tuition.

Requirements: A minimum high school GPA of 3.5 (on a 4.0 scale)

P.S: Applicants will experience an interview and complete an essay for scholarship consideration.

Application Deadline: December 1

Application link: https://www.capital.edu/admission/tuition-and-financial-aid/first-year-student-scholarships/

12 John Carroll University

Location: University Heights, Ohio
Setting: Suburban (62 Acres)
Undergraduate Enrollment: 2,660
Type: Private

Ignatian Heritage Scholarship: Awards up to the full cost of tuition.

Eligibility: First-year students applying for admission from Catholic, Jesuit, and/or Cristo Rey High Schools are eligible to apply.

Requirements: Top Applicants.

Say Yes Scholarship: Awards Full tuition and fees.

Eligibility: This scholarship is available to students attending Say Yes eligible schools in Cleveland, OH.

Castellano Scholarship: Awards Full tuition.

Eligibility: This scholarship is available to students who has studied Latin at the secondary level for at least three years and intends to major in Classical Languages at JCU.

Father Hurtado Scholarship: Awards up to Full tuition.

Eligibility: This scholarship is awarded to an incoming first-year student from St. Martin de Porres High School in Cleveland, OH.

Learn more: https://www.jcu.edu/sefs/financing-jcu-education/new-first-year-sefs/donor-scholarships-sefs

Application Deadline: December 1

Application link: https://www.jcu.edu/sefs/financing-jcu-education/new-first-year-sefs/new-first-year-student-scholarships-sefs

13 Shawnee State University

Location: Portsmouth, Ohio
Setting: City (62 Acres)
Undergraduate Enrollment: 3,023
Type: Public

Shawnee Scholar Award: Awards Full tuition.

Requirements: A minimum ACT score of 30 or SAT (combined reading/math) score of 1320+ and a high school GPA of at least 3.8/4.0 scale.

Free – Tuition Program: The award provides free undergraduate tuition for qualifying incoming freshmen.

Eligibility: Applicants must qualify for Federal Pell Grant (as determined by the FAFSA) | Residents of Scioto, Lawrence, Adams, Pike, Jackson or Ross Counties in Ohio; or Greenup, Boyd or Lewis Counties in Kentucky.

Requirements: A minimum high school GPA of 3.0 | ACT score of at least 18

Check here for more details: https://www.shawnee.edu/free-tuition

Choose Ohio First Computer Engineering Technology Scholarship: Award ranges from $1,500 up to Full tuition.

14 University of Mount Union

Location: Alliance, Ohio
Setting: City (123 Acres)
Undergraduate Enrollment: 1,891
Type: Private

Investment Alliance Scholarship: Awards Full tuition.

Eligibility: Awarded to the top 15 students of each Alliance High School graduating class, as identified by the school district.

Requirements: Top Applicants.

Presidential Scholarship: Awards Full tuition.

Requirements: A GPA of at least 3.75 or a GPA of at least 3.6 combined with a minimum ACT score of 30 or SAT score of 1360 (EBRW+Math) Learn more: https://www.mountunion.edu/psp-apply

Application Deadline: November 8

Application link: https://www.mountunion.edu/scholarships-and-grants

Choose Ohio First Nursing Scholarship: Award ranges from $1,500 up to Full tuition.

Learn more: https://www.shawnee.edu/nursing-scholarship

Application Deadline: February 1

Application link: https://www.shawnee.edu/financial-aid/scholarships

15 Walsh University

Location: North Canton, Ohio
Setting: Suburban (143 Acres)
Undergraduate Enrollment: 1,639
Type: Private

Walsh University Presidential Scholarship: Awards Full tuition.

Requirements: Top Applicants.

Walsh University Founders' Scholarship: Awards Full tuition.

Requirements: Top Applicants.

Check site for more details…

Application Deadline: December 1

Application link: https://www.walsh.edu/scholarships-and-grants.html

16 Bowling Green State University

Location: Bowling Green, Ohio
Setting: Rural (1,338 Acres)
Undergraduate Enrollment: 14,465
Type: Public

Presidential Scholars Award: Awards Full in state tuition and fees.

Requirements: 3.8 cumulative high school GPA on a 4.0 scale | 30 ACT composite score or 1390 SAT (Evidence-Based Reading and Writing)

Alumni Laureate Scholarship: Awards Full in state tuition, fees and a $1,000 book award.

Requirements: 3.5 cumulative high school GPA on a 4.0 scale | 27 ACT composite score or 1280 SAT, Please refer to this site for more details: https://www.bgsu.edu/admissions/scholarships-and-financial-aid.html

Forsyth Award: Awards Full in state tuition and fees.

Requirements: Top Applicants.

Sidney A. Ribeau President's Leadership Academy: Awards Full in state tuition and fees.

Requirements: Top Applicants.

Application Deadline: December 1

Application link: https://www.bgsu.edu/honors-college/applying/scholarships-and-awards.html

17 Wilmington College

Location: Wilmington, Ohio
Setting: Rural (65 Acres)
Undergraduate Enrollment: 1,165
Type: Private

Presidential Scholarship: Awards Full tuition.

Requirements: 3.5 – 4.0 cumulative GPA | 25 – 36 ACT composite score (1200 minimum New SAT critical reading and math combined score)

Application Deadline: February 15

Application link:
https://www.wilmington.edu/admission/financial-aid/scholarships-awards/

18 Denison University

Location: Granville, Ohio
Setting: Suburban (850 Acres)
Undergraduate Enrollment: 2,272
Type: Private

Denison annually offers several merit scholarships to first-year students, and scholarships generally range from $5,000 to *full tuition*.

Check site for more details…

Application Deadline: December 1

Application link:
https://denison.edu/campus/finances/types-of-scholarships-aid

19 Miami University

Location: Oxford, Ohio
Setting: Rural (2,100 Acres)
Undergraduate Enrollment: 16,977
Type: Private

Ohio's Governor's Scholarship: Awards Full tuition.

Requirements: Scholarship is awarded to top student from each of Ohio's 8 counties.

Application Deadline: December 1

Application link:
https://miamioh.edu/admission/merit-scholarships/

20 Otterbein University

Location: Westerville, Ohio
Setting: Suburban (140 Acres)
Undergraduate Enrollment: 2,253
Type: Private

Tuition Exchange Scholarship: Awards up to Full tuition.

Requirements: Top Applicants. Please refer to this site for more details: https://telo.tuitionexchange.org/schools.cfm

Full Tuition Scholarships: Otterbein awards three *full tuition scholarships* through an essay competition.

P.S: By invitation only.

Requirements: Top Applicants.

Application Deadline: December 15

Application link: https://www.otterbein.edu/financial-aid/scholarships/#admission

21 Muskingum University

Location: New Concord, Ohio
Setting: Rural (245 Acres)
Undergraduate Enrollment: 1,578
Type: Private

John Glenn Scholarship: Awards Full tuition.

Requirements: Top Applicants.

Check site for more details…

Application Deadline: November 1

Application link: https://www.muskingum.edu/financial-aid/first-year

22 Oberlin College

Location: Oberlin, Ohio
Setting: Suburban (440 Acres)
Undergraduate Enrollment: 2,942
Type: Private

Robinson Scholarship: Awards Full tuition.

P.S: This scholarship program is awarded to graduates of Oberlin High School.

Eligibility: Applicants must have resided in the Oberlin School District for at least four years prior to high school graduation, must have attended Oberlin High School for four years, and must continue residence in the area while enrolled at Oberlin College.

Requirements: Top Applicants.

Scholarships for International Students

Eduardo Chivambo Mondlane Scholarship: Awards Full tuition scholarship for up to four years.

Eligibility: Any citizen from a **sub-Saharan African country** who is applying to Oberlin College of Arts and Sciences is eligible.

Edwin O. Reischauer Scholarship: Awards Full tuition scholarship for up to four years.

23 Bluffton University

Location: Bluffton, Ohio
Setting: Rural (235 Acres)
Undergraduate Enrollment: 728
Type: Private

Presidential Scholarship: Awards Full tuition.

Requirements: A minimum 3.5 High School GPA | 24 ACT/1160 SAT (or higher)

Scholarships Available for Intervention specialist coursework

Full tuition scholarships will be awarded to select teachers to earn intervention specialist endorsements. Grants will be presented to 11 teachers from Education Partner schools.

Application Deadline: November 1

Application link:
https://www.bluffton.edu/admissions/financialaid/scholarships/index.aspx

---

Eligibility: Any **Japanese national** who has been accepted for admission to the Oberlin College of Arts and Sciences is eligible for this award.

Application Deadline: November 15

Application link:
https://www.oberlin.edu/financial-aid/basics/scholarships-offered

24

Wright State University

Location: Fairborn, Ohio
Setting: Suburban (651 Acres)
Undergraduate Enrollment: 7,477
Type: Public

Rowdy Raider Scholarship: Award range from $1,000 to the value of in-state tuition.

Requirements: Top Applicants.

ArtsGala Scholarship Department of Music: The award amount ranges from $500 to the value of in-state tuition.

Music Scholarship: The award amount ranges from $500 to the value of in-state tuition.

Eligibility: Based on audition results with the School of Music.

ArtsGala Scholarship Department of Theatre, Dance, and Motion Pictures: The award amount ranges from $500 to the value of in-state tuition.

Eligibility: Based on audition/interview with Department of Theatre, Dance, and Motion Pictures.

Dayton Ballet 11 & Dayton Contemporary Dance Company 11 Scholarships: The award amount ranges from $500 to the value of in-state tuition.

Eligibility: Based on audition/interview with Department of Theatre, Dance, and Motion Pictures.

P.S: Applicant must provide a DVD with B.F.A Admission/Scholarship Applications.

Theatre Arts Talent Scholarships; Tom Hanks Scholarship; Augsburger/Estevez Scholarship (Martin Sheen): The award amount ranges from $500 to the value of in-state tuition.

Eligibility: Based on audition with Department of Theatre, Dance, and Motion Pictures.

Application Deadline: November 1

Application link: https://www.wright.edu/raiderconnect/financial-aid/first-year-scholarships#about

1   Oklahoma State University

Location: Stillwater, Oklahoma
Setting: City (1,489 Acres)
Undergraduate Enrollment: 20,197
Type: Public

In-State Scholarships

Cowboy Covenant – An Oklahoma's Promise Partnership: Awards Full tuition (Oklahoma's Promise) and a $1,000 stipend for four years.

Requirements: Applicant must be an Oklahoma resident | Must enroll in the 8th, 9th, 10th or 11th grade | Parents' federal adjusted gross income must not exceed $60k per year.

Application Deadline: November 1

Application link:
https://go.okstate.edu/scholarships-financial-aid/types-of-aid/scholarships-and-grants/freshman-scholarships/

2   Oklahoma Christian University

Location: Edmond, Oklahoma
Setting: City (200 Acres)
Undergraduate Enrollment: 1,877
Type: Private

Ike's Promise: Awards Full tuition.

Requirements: ACT score of 20+ or SAT of 1020+ or CLT of 66 plus | FAFSA EFC of <$1,000 or full Pell Grant recipient or Oklahoma's Promise scholarship. Please refer to this site for more details: https://www.oc.edu/ikes-promise

Oklahoma Christian University Difference Maker Scholarship

Tier 2 – EPIC Presidential Award: Awards Full tuition.

P.S: A Difference Maker applicant will be chosen to receive the EPIC Presidential Award for a four-year, full-tuition scholarship.

Application Deadline: December 1

Application link:
https://www.oc.edu/admissions/financial-services/scholarships

3

Oklahoma Baptist University

Location: Shawnee, Oklahoma
Setting: City (300 Acres)
Undergraduate Enrollment: 1,430
Type: Private

Full Tuition Scholarships

University Scholar: Awards Full tuition.

Requirements: High School GPA of at least 3.5 | ACT of at least 29 or an SAT score of at least 1330 or CLT of at least 97 | A Letter of recommendation attesting to your academic accomplishments | Current resume exhibiting leadership, involvement in school, church, community, and work activities | 500 – 1,000 word essay.

Check site for more details…

Allen Academic Scholar: Awards Full tuition.

Requirements: High School GPA of at least 3.5 | ACT of at least 27 or an SAT score of at least 1260 (Critical Reading and Math only)

Martin Academic Scholar: Awards Full tuition.

Eligibility: Applicants must be Choctaw Indian with a degree of Indian blood recognized by the Choctaw Nation and Oklahoma residents.

Requirements: A cumulative High School GPA of at least 3.0 | ACT of at least 25 or an SAT score of at least 1200 (Critical Reading and Math only)

Application Deadline: January 1

Application link: https://www.okbu.edu/financial-aid/scholarships-and-grants.html

4 University of Tulsa

Location: Tulsa, Oklahoma
Setting: City (209 Acres)
Undergraduate Enrollment: 2,728
Type: Private

Presidential Scholars: Awards Full tuition.

Requirements: Applicants *must meet one or more of the following requirements*: National Merit Semi-finalist's who list The University of Tulsa as School of Choice with National Merit Scholarship Corporation | National Hispanic Scholars who rank in the top 10% of their graduating class | Rank in the top 5% of their graduating class OR Have at least a 4.0 weighted GPA.

Application Deadline: January 15

Application link: https://utulsa.edu/financial-aid/scholarships/presidential-scholarship/

5 Southwestern Christian University

Location: Bethany, Oklahoma
Setting: Suburban (10 Acres)
Undergraduate Enrollment: 460
Type: Private

National Merit Scholar: Awards Full tuition.

Requirements: 31+ ACT/SAT equivalent.

Application Deadline: October 15

Application link: https://swcu.edu/admissions/financial-assistance/scholarships-and-discounts

6 Oklahoma Wesleyan University

Location: Bartlesville, Oklahoma
Setting: Suburban (35 Acres)
Undergraduate Enrollment: 791
Type: Private

Valedictorian Scholarship: Awards Full tuition.

Eligibility: OKWU offers 100% tuition to the Valedictorian of accredited high schools; some restrictions may apply.

National Merit Scholarship: Awards Full tuition to National Merit Finalist.

Eligibility: Applicant must be a National Merit Finalist.

Application Deadline: January 15

Application link:
https://www.okwu.edu/admissions/financial-aid/traditional/

7 University of Central Oklahoma

Location: Edmond, Oklahoma
Setting: Suburban (210 Acres)
Undergraduate Enrollment: 11,834
Type: Public

Oklahoma State Regents of Higher Education Scholarships

Oklahoma Academic Scholar Program: Awards Full tuition and $4,000 cash per year.

Requirements: 99.5 percntile on National ACT/SAT

Academic Scholar Institutional Nominee Program: Awards Full tuition and $2,400 cash per year.

Eligibility: Applicant must be an Oklahoma resident.

Requirements: Achieve one of the following: 30 on national ACT/SAT OR 3.8 unweighted GPA and rank in the Top 4% of graduating class.

OSRHE Baccalaureate Scholarship: Awards Full tuition and $3,000 cash per year.

Eligibility: Applicant must be an Oklahoma resident.

Requirements: A mimimum 3.5 unweighted high school GPA | Minimum 30 ACT on national ACT test.

Application Deadline: February 1

Application link: https://www.uco.edu/admissions-aid/financial-aid/scholarships/

8

University of Science & Arts of Oklahoma

Location: Chickasha, Oklahoma
Setting: Rural (75 Acres)
Undergraduate Enrollment: 846
Type: Public

Scholarships for In-State Student's

Academic Scholars Program: Awards $15,280 per year. (This covers the cost of tuition and course related fees for in-state students)

Requirements: Applicant must be named a Presidential Scholar by the U.S. Department of Education | Named a National Merit Scholar or National Merit finalist | Scoring in the 99th percentile on a national ACT.

Regional University Baccalaureate Scholarship: Awards $15,280 per year. (This covers the cost of tuition and course related fees for in-state students)

Requirements: Applicant must be an Oklahoma resident and a U.S. citizen | Minimum national ACT composite score of 30 and a minimum 3.50 GPA on a 4.0 scale.

Regent's Academic Scholar (Institutional Nominee): Award amount covers the cost of tuition and course related fees.

Requirements: Applicant must be an Oklahoma resident and a U.S. citizen | Minimum national ACT composite score of 30 or SAT equivalent and a minimum 3.50 GPA on a 4.0 scale | Rank in the top 4% of their high school class.

Application Deadline: December 1

Application link: https://usao.edu/financial-aid/financial-aid-options/scholarships.html

9

Oklahoma City University

★ 1904 - 2004 ★
OKLAHOMA CITY UNIVERSITY

Location: Oklahoma City, Oklahoma
Setting: Urban (104 Acres)
Undergraduate Enrollment: 1,430
Type: Private

The Meinders Business Leadership Fellows Program: Awards range up to Full tuition.

Eligibility: Awarded to top applicants entering the *Meinders School of Business at Oklahoma City University.*

Requirements: An ACT score of 28+ (or an SAT equivalent)

Frank G. Brooks Memorial Scholarship: Awards Full tuition.

Eligibility: Awarded to outstanding first-year student who chooses to study biology at Oklahoma City University.

Requirements: Top Applicants | A letter of recommendation from a teacher or mentor, community involvement, and an application essay.

Computer Science Fellows Program: Awards range up to Full tuition.

Eligibility: Awarded to top applicants entering the *Computer Science program at Oklahoma City University.*

Requirements: A minimum high school cumulative GPA of 3.60

Pre-Engineering B.S. Studies Scholarship: Awards Full tuition.

P.S: Oklahoma City University students wishing to become engineers can do so through the Bachelor's and Master's Degree in Engineering partnership with Washington University in St. Louis. Check site for more details…

Requirements: An ACT science and math scores of 27 (or SAT Math score of 640)

Bishop's Scholars Award: Awards Full tuition.

Requirements: The Applicant should hold membership in a United Methodist Church | Obtain recommendation from the senior pastor or youth minister of the student's church.

Application Deadline: March 1

Application link:
https://www.okcu.edu/financialaid/types-of-assistance/scholarships/freshmen

Portland State University

1

Location: Portland, Oregon
Setting: Urban (50 Acres)
Undergraduate Enrollment: 17,753
Type: Public

Scholarships for Oregon Residents

Four Years Free: Award covers base tuition and mandatory fees for up to four years.

Eligibility: Awarded to Oregon residents.

Requirements: Top Applicants.

Transfers Finish Free: Award covers base tuition and mandatory fees for up to four years.

Eligibility: Awarded to qualified incoming transfer students | Oregon residents.

Requirements: Top Applicants.

Application Deadline: June 15

Application link:
https://www.pdx.edu/student-finance/scholarships

Linfield University

2

Location: McMinnville, Oregon
Setting: Rural (189 Acres)
Undergraduate Enrollment: 1,283
Type: Private

Linfield Merit Award

National Merit Scholarship Corporation Program: Award amounts range from half-tuition on a no-need basis, to **Full tuition** with sufficient financial need.

Eligibility: Awarded to students who are finalists in the National Merit Scholarship Corporation Program, and who list Linfield as their first choice college.

Application Deadline: October 1

Application link:
https://www.linfield.edu/financial-aid/incoming-students/mcminnville-students/first-year-scholarships.html

1 Villanova University

Location: Villanova, Pennsylvania
Setting: Suburban (260 Acres)
Undergraduate Enrollment: 7,032
Type: Private

Presidential Scholarship: Full tuition, room, board (up to 21 meals per week plan), general fee, and the cost of textbooks for eight consecutive semesters.

Criteria: In order to be considered for the presidential Scholarship, students must first be nominated by the chief academic officer of their high school (principal, president, headmaster), secondary school counselor, or an official school designee.

2 Elizabethtown College

Location: Elizabethtown, Pennsylvania
Setting: Suburban (203 Acres)
Undergraduate Enrollment: 1,691
Type: Private

Stamps Scholarship: Award covers full tuition as well as an enrichment fund which is funded by the Strive Foundation and Elizabethtown College.

Eligibility: Top Applicants.

Application Deadline: January 15

Application link:
https://www.etown.edu/admissions/financial-aid/index.aspx

St. Martin de Porres Scholarship: Full tuition and general fees.

Eligibility: U.S. citizens or permanent residents from one or more of the most underrepresented groups at the Villanova University.

Anthony Randazzo Endowed Presidential Scholarship: Full tuition, room, board (up to 21 meals per week plan), general fee, and the cost of textbooks for eight consecutive semesters.

Eligibility: Awarded to a first year African American/Black student | Applicant must reside in the city of Philadelphia, Pennsylvania.

Application Deadline: January 2

Application link: https://www1.villanova.edu/university/undergraduate-admission/Financial-Assistance-and-scholarship/merit-based-scholarships.html

3 Gannon University

Location: Erie, Pennsylvania
Setting: City (63 Acres)
Undergraduate Enrollment: 3,165
Type: Private

Presidential Scholarship: 100% tuition for all four (4) years.

Requirements: Top of admission pool academically.

Application Deadline: December 1

Application link:
https://www.gannon.edu/Financial-Aid/Types-of-Financial-Aid/Gannon-Scholarships-and-Awards/

4 Gwynedd Mercy University

Location: Gwynedd Valley, Pennsylvania
Setting: Suburban (160 Acres)
Undergraduate Enrollment: 1,792
Type: Private

Presidential Scholarship: Full tuition for all four (4) years.

Requirements: Strong academic record with a GPA of at least 3.75

Application Deadline: Contact Admission Office.

Application link:
https://www.gmercyu.edu/admissions-aid/financial-aid-tuition/types-aid/scholarships/

5 King's College

Location: Wilkes-Barre, Pennsylvania
Setting: City (33 Acres)
Undergraduate Enrollment: 1,831
Type: Private

Army & Airforce ROTC: Scholarships covers full tuition, fees and monthly stipends.

Requirements: Contact Admission Office.

Application Deadline: Contact Admission Office.

Application link:
https://www.kings.edu/admissions/financial_aid/scholarships_and_fa_programs/scholarships

6 University of Pittsburgh

Location: Pittsburgh, Pennsylvania
Setting: Urban (145 Acres)
Undergraduate Enrollment: 19,980
Type: Public

Nordenberg Scholars Program: The scholarship covers full tuition for all four (4) years.

Requirements: Pennsylvania residency | U.S. Citizen or Permanent Resident | Complete Nordenberg Scholars application

Application Deadline: December 1

Application link:
https://financialaid.pitt.edu/types-of-aid/scholarships/

7 Misericordia University

Location: Dallas, Pennsylvania
Setting: Suburban (129 Acres)
Undergraduate Enrollment: 1,775
Type: Private

Sr. Mary Glennon '62 Scholarships: Scholarship offers 100% tuition for all four (4) years.

Requirements: Good academic record with a 3.7 GPA or top 5 percent of graduating class.

Application Deadline: December 15

Application link: https://www.misericordia.edu/financial-aid/scholarship/sr-mary-glennon-scholarships

8 Saint Joseph's University

Location: Philadelphia, Pennsylvania
Setting: Suburban (125 Acres)
Undergraduate Enrollment: 4,196
Type: Private

Johm P. Mcnulty Scholars Program: Full tuition for all four (4) years.

Requirements: Strong academic record (3.5+/4.00 High school GPA) | Women who declare major in biology, chemistry, environmental science, physics, mathematics or computer science.

Application Deadline: January 28

Application link: https://www.sju.edu/mcnulty-scholars

9 Cedar Crest College

Location: Allentown, Pennsylvania
Setting: Suburban (85 Acres)
Undergraduate Enrollment: 1,053
Type: Private

Cedar Crest Scholarship: Award covers full tuition for all four (4) years.

Requirements: Excellent academic and extracurricular record.

Application Deadline: Contact Admission Office.

Application link: https://www.cedarcrest.edu/stufinserv/traditionalscholarships.shtm

10 Temple University

Location: Philadelphia, Pennsylvania
Setting: Urban (406 Acres)
Undergraduate Enrollment: 25,967
Type: Public

Army/Airforce ROTC: 100% tuition for all four (4) years.

Requirements: At least a 2.5 High school GPA | Physically fit | 1100 SAT (Airforce ROTC)

Application Deadline: Contact Admission Office.

Application link:
https://sfs.temple.edu/financial-aid-types/scholarships/new-incoming-students

11 Saint Vincent College

Location: Latrobe, Pennsylvania
Setting: Suburban (200 Acres)
Undergraduate Enrollment: 1,430
Type: Private

Wimmer Scholarship: Full tuition for all four (4) years.

Requirements: A high school GPA of 3.75 or higher and an SAT of 1300 and above (OR ACT score of 28 | OR CLT of 86)

Application Deadline: February 15

Application link:
https://www.stvincent.edu/admission-aid/wimmer-scholarship-competition.html

12 Messiah College

Location: Mechanicsburg, Pennsylvania
Setting: Suburban (471 Acres)
Undergraduate Enrollment: 2,495
Type: Private

Trustees' Scholarship: Scholarship award covers full tuition.

Requirements: A good academic record of at least 3.4 high school GPA and 1320 SAT (OR 29 ACT OR 88-91 ACT)

Application Deadline: February 1

Application link:
https://www.messiah.edu/honorsscholarships

13 Robert Morris University

Location: Moon Township, Pennsylvania
Setting: Suburban (230 Acres)
Undergraduate Enrollment: 3,007
Type: Private

Presidential Scholarship: 100% tuition for all four (4) years.

Requirements: Candidates should have excellent academic records.

Application Deadline: Contaact Admission Office.

Application link:
https://www.rmu.edu/admissions/financial-aid/scholarships#institutional

14 Keystone College

Location: Factoryville, Pennsylvania
Setting: Rural (276 Acres)
Undergraduate Enrollment: 1,171
Type: Private

Academic Excellence Scholarship: Full tuition for all four (4) years.

Requirements: Strong academic record (high school GPA and test scores inclusive)

Application Deadline: February 1

Application link:
https://www.keystone.edu/admissions/tuition-aid/scholarships/

15 DeSales University

Location: Center Valley, Pennsylvania
Setting: Suburban (550 Acres)
Undergraduate Enrollment: 2,309
Type: Private

Leadership Scholarship: Award covers 100% tuition for all four (4) years.

Requirements: Outstanding Leadership and satisfactory academic record.

Application Deadline: December 1

Application link:
https://www.desales.edu/admissions-financial-aid/undergraduate-admissions-aid/financial-aid-scholarships/desales-scholarships/leadership-scholarship-(6-full-tuition-scholarships)

16 La Salle University

Location: Philadelphia, Pennsylvania

Setting: Urban (133 Acres)

Undergraduate Enrollment: 2,746

Type: Private

Christian Brothers' Scholarship: Full tuition for all four (4) years.

Requirements: Excellent Academic Record like Top 10% of graduating class.

Application Deadline: January 15

Application link:
https://www.lasalle.edu/financialaid/scholarships/christian-brothers-scholarship/

17 Harrisburg University of Science and Technology

Location: Harrisburg, Pennsylvania

Setting: Urban (38,000 square-foot)

Undergraduate Enrollment: 637

Type: Private

Harrisburg Partnership Scholarship: 100% tuition for all four (4) years.

Requirements: Student from Harrsiburg School District | Contact admission office for more information.

Application Deadline: May 1

Application link:
https://www.harrisburgu.edu/tuition-financial-aid/financial-aid/hu-scholarships-and-grants/

18

Drexel University

Location: Philadelphia, Pennsylvania
Setting: Urban (96 Acres)
Undergraduate Enrollment: 12,834
Type: Private

Drexel Athletic Scholarships Award covers full tuition for all four (4) years.

Requirements: Contact the athletic department.

Drexel Global Scholar Program: Awards 100% tuition for all four (4) years.

Requirements: International freshmen | Satisfactory academic performance and leadership capacity.

Application Deadline: November 15

Drexel Liberty Scholars: Awards covers full tuition and fees for all four (4) years.

Requirements: US Citizen/Permanent Resident with demonstrated financial need (Using CSS/FAFSA)

Application Deadline: November 1

Army/Navy ROTC Scholarship: This scholarship covers 100% tuition for all four (4) years.

Requirements: Army/Navy ROTC Cadets enrolled at Drexel.

Application Deadline: Contact admission office.

Application link: https://drexel.edu/drexelcentral/finaid/grants/undergraduate-scholarships/

19 Kutztown University

Location: Kutztown, Pennsylvania
Setting: Rural (289 Acres)
Undergraduate Enrollment: 6,697
Type: Public

Merit Scholarships: Awards up to full tuition.

Requirements: Top Applicants.

Sesquicentennial Academic Honors Scholarship: 100% tuition for all four (4) years.

Requirements: Students should have a high school GPA of at least 3.5 and a minimum SAT score of 1410 (OR 31 ACT)

Board of Governors Scholarship: Awards covers 100% tuition for all four (4) years.

Requirements: Top Applicants.

Application Deadline: March 1

Application link:
https://www.kutztown.edu/affordability/guide-to-financial-aid/scholarships.html

20 University of Scranton

Location: Scranton, Pennsylvania
Setting: City (58 Acres)
Undergraduate Enrollment: 3,487
Type: Private

Presidential Scholarship: Scholarship covers full tuition for four (4) academic years.

Requirements: Strong Academic and extracurricular record.

Army ROTC Scholarship: Scholarships covers full tuition, $1,200 for books and monthly stipends.

Requirements: Contact Admission Office.

Application Deadline: Contact Admission Office.

Application link:
https://www.scranton.edu/financial-aid/merit-based-sch.shtml

21 # Lehigh University

Location: Bethlehem, Pennsylvania
Setting: City (2,355 Acres)
Undergraduate Enrollment: 5,451
Type: Private

Founder's and Trustees' Scholarships: These scholarships covers full or half tution for all four (4) years.

Requirements: Student should in the top tier of applicant pool.

Application Deadline: Contact Admission Office.

Application link: https://www1.lehigh.edu/admissions/merit-scholarships

22 # Rosemont College

Location: Rosemont, Pennsylvania
Setting: Suburban (56 Acres)
Undergraduate Enrollment: 480
Type: Private

Cornelian Scholarship: Award covers full tuition and fees for four (4) years.

Requirements: Strong Academic and extracurricular record – with high school GPA of 3.25 or higher.

Application Deadline: January 18

Application link: https://www.rosemont.edu/admissions/tuition-and-aid/pdf/undergrad-final-aid-brochure.pdf

1 University of Rhode Island

Location: Kingstown, Rhode Island
Settting: Rural (1,245 Acres)
Undergraduate Enrollment: 13,928
Type: Public

Thomas M. Ryan Scholars Program: Awards Full tuition, fees, housing, dining, books, and one Global winter travel J term experience with faculty.

Requirements: Top Applicants.

Alfred J. Verrecchia Business Scholars Program: Awards Full tuition, fees, housing, dining, books, and one Global winter travel J term experience with faculty.

Requirements: Awarded to selected students interested in majoring in Business.

Application Deadline: June 26

2 Providence College

Location: Providence, Rhode Island
Setting: City (105 Acres)
Undergraduate Enrollment: 4,245
Type: Private

Roddy Scholarship: Awards Full tuition, fees, room and board.

Requirements: Applicants must aspire to a career in the medical profession | Consideration is based on outstanding academic achievement in high school | Awarded to first-year students who reside in the United States.

Application link: https://financial-aid.providence.edu/types-of-assistance/institutional-merit-based/

URI Narragansett Undergraduate Scholarship: Awards up to full in-tuition and fees, plus $5,000

Requirements: Accepted into URI | Have an official FAFSA on file | A tribal enrollment ID card or an official letter from the tribal administration that confirms membership through a direct family member (parents)

Application Deadline: Contact the ROTC Department for scholarship deadline dates.

Application link: https://web.uri.edu/admission/scholarships/

3

Roger Williams University

Location: Bristol, Rhode Island
Setting: Suburban (140 Acres)
Undergraduate Enrollment: 4,206
Type: Private

Intercultural Leadership Ambassador Program & Scholarship: 100% tuition for all four (4) years.

Requirements: Student must have a 3.0+ GPA and demonstrate go co-curriclar involvements

Harold Payson Memorial Scholarship: 100% tuition for all four (4) years.

Requirements: Student must has resided in Bristol for at least two years | For U.S. Citizens and Permanent Residents Only.

Michael Andrade Memorial Scholarship: 100% tuition and fees for all four (4) years.

Requirements: Student must be a graduate of Mount Hope High School | Have a B averageand an SAT of 1000 +(OR ACT equivalent) | For U.S. Citizens and Permanent Residents Only.

Porthsmouth High School (RI) Scholarship: 100% tuition for all four (4) years.

Requirements: Student must be a graduate of Portsmouth High School (RI) | Have a 3.0+ GPA and an SAT of 1000+ (OR ACT equivalent) | For U.S. Citizens and Permanent Residents Only.

Application Deadline: Contact Admission Office.

Application link: https://catalog.rwu.edu/content.php?catoid=3&navoid=124

1 South Carolina State University

Location: Orangeburg, South Carolina

Setting: Suburban (160 Acres)

Undergraduate Enrollment: 2,074

Type: Public

General University Scholarship: 100% tuition for all four (4) years.

Requirements: High school GPA of at least 3.25 | SAT score of 1100+(OR 24 in ACT)

SC State University Achievers Scholarship: 100% tuition for all four (4) years.

Requirements: Student must already be enrolled on SC State | Achieve a GPA of at least 3.5

Application Deadline: Contact Admissions Office.

Application link: https://www2.scsu.edu/scholarships/institutionalscholarships.aspx

Application Deadline: Contact Admissions Office.

Application link: https://anderson.edu/blog/honors-program-scholarship/

2 Furman University

Location: Greenville, South Carolina

Setting: Suburban (800 Acres)

Undergraduate Enrollment: 2,304

Type: Private

ROTC Scholarships: Awards up to full tuition and fees.

Requirements: Top Applicants.

Application Deadline: Contact the ROTC Department for scholarship deadline dates.

Application link: https://www.furman.edu/financial-aid/aid-types/other-scholarships/

3 Anderson University

Location: Anderson, South Carolina

Setting: City (385 Acres)

Undergraduate Enrollment: 3,157

Type: Private

Honors Program Scholarship: 100% tuition for all four (4) years.

Requirements: High school GPA of at least 3.75 | Good test scores | Must accepted into the Anderson University Honors Program.

1 University of South Dakota

Location: Vermillion, South Dakota
Setting: Rural (274 Acres)
Undergraduate Enrollment: 6,987
Type: Public

Presidential Alumni Scholarship: Award covers 100% in-state tuition and fees for all four (4) years.

Requirements: Excellent Academic & Extracurricular performance. Contact Admission Office for more info.

Walter A. & Lucy Yoshiko Buhler Scholarship: Award covers 100% in-state tuition and fees for all four (4) years.

Requirements: Excellent Academic & Extracurricular performance | Enrolled in a Business or Fine Arts major | Contact Admission Office for more info.

Application Deadline: December 1

Application link: https://www.usd.edu/Admissions-and-Aid/Financial-Aid/Types-of-Aid/Scholarships

2 University of Sioux Falls

Location: Sioux Falls, South Dakota
Setting: City (140 Acres)
Undergraduate Enrollment: 1,337
Type: Private

National Merit Scholarship: This Scholarships covers full tuition for four (4) complete years.

Requirements: Applicant must be a national merit scholar.

Application Deadline: Contact Admission Office.

Application link: https://www.usiouxfalls.edu/financial-aid/university-scholarships

1 Belmont University

Location: Nashville, Tennessee
Setting: Urban (93 Acres)
Undergraduate Enrollment: 7,069
Type: Private

Ingram Diversity Leadership Scholarship: This prestigious award covers full tuition for all four (4) years.

Requirements: Student must be from Nashville area | High academic performance and good participation in extracurriccular activities.

E.S. Rose Scholarship: This prestigious award covers full tuition for all four (4) years.

Requirements: Student must live in proximity to E.S. Rose Park in Nashville | High academic performance and good participation in extracurriccular activities.

Application Deadline: December 1

Application link:
https://www.belmont.edu/sfs/scholarships/merit.html

2 Middle Tennessee State University

Location: Murfreesboro, Tennessee
Setting: CIty (550 Acres)
Undergraduate Enrollment: 17,892
Type: Public

The Buchanan Fellowship: Award covers full tuition for complete four (4) years.

Requirements: Student is expected to have a high school GPA of 3.5 or higher and an SAT of 1360+ (or ACT equivalent)

Application Deadline: December 1

Application link:
https://www.mtsu.edu/honors/buchanan/index.php

3 Milligan University

Location: Milligan, Tennessee
Setting: Suburban (355 Acres)
Undergraduate Enrollment: 789
Type: Private

Jeanes Honors Scholarships: This scholarship offer covers 100% tuition for all four (4) years.

Requirements: High school GPA of 3.5 or higher | 1300+ SAT (28+ ACT, 86+ CLT) | Active participation in ecxtracurrcicular activities.

Application Deadline: December 1

Application link:
https://www.milligan.edu/programs/honors-program/

4 Maryville College

Location: Maryville, Tennessee
Setting: City (300 Acres)
Undergraduate Enrollment: 1,046
Type: Private

McGill Scholarship/Fellowship: Awards up to Full tuition for all four (4) years.

Requirements: 3.7+ GPA | 1390+ SAT(28+ ACT OR 92+ CLT) | Demonstarted Leadership Abilities.

Application Deadline: January 28

Application link:
https://www.maryvillecollege.edu/admissions/finaid/types-of-aid/scholarships-awards/mcgill/

5 Bryan College

Location: Dayton, Tennessee
Setting: Rural (128 Acres)
Undergraduate Enrollment: 1,390
Type: Private

Bryan Opportunity Scholarship Program: Award covers full tuition for all four (4) years.

Requirements: Applicant(s) must be a first-time freshman | Complete FAFSA by January 31 | Total family income < $36,000 | GPA of 3.0 and ACT 21 or SAT 1060.

Application Deadline: January 31

Application link:
https://www.bryan.edu/scholarship/bryan-opportunity-scholarship-program/

6 Vanderbilt University

Location: Nashville, Tennessee
Setting: Urban (333 Acres)
Undergraduate Enrollment: 7,111
Type: Private

Ingram Scholars Program: This scholarship offer covers 100% tuition for all four(4) years, plus a one-time summer stipend.

Application link:
https://www.vanderbilt.edu/scholarships/ingram.php

Cornelius Vanderbilt Scholarship: This scholarship offer covers 100% tuition for all four(4) years, plus a one-time summer stipend.

P.S: Vanderbilt will provide additional need-based financial aid to those Cornelius Vanderilt Scholarship recipient whose demonstrated needs exceeds the amount of full tuition.

Requirements: Student must have excellent academics and extracurricular record.

Application Deadline: December 1

Application link:
https://www.vanderbilt.edu/scholarships/signature.php

7 Southern Adventist University

Location: Collegedale, Tennessee
Setting: Rural (1,000 Acres)
Undergraduate Enrollment: 2,400
Type: Private

Freshman Academic Scholarship: Award covers full tuition.

Freshman Full Tuition Scholarship: Award covers full tuition.

Requirements: Score a minimum of 7,301 points.

To get points: (1) Multiply your high school GPA (over/4.0) by 1000 | (2) Multiply your ACT test score by 100 | (3) Add all points from Step 1 and 2.

P.S: Check site for more details in regards to converting your SAT score to an ACT score in respect of this scholarship(s).

National Merit Scholarship: Covers Full tuition.

Requirements: Applicant must be a National Merit Finalist, accepted in the National Hispanic Recognition Program (Hispanic students) or National Achievement Scholarship Program (African American students)

Application link:
https://www.southern.edu/undergrad/finances/grants-and-scholarships.html

8 Lipscomb University

Location: Nashville, Tennessee
Setting: Suburban (113 Acres)
Undergraduate Enrollment: 2,952
Type: Private

Trustee Scholarship: 100% tuition for all four (4) years.

Requirements: Candidates should have a GPA of 3.5 or higher and an SAT score of 1360 or better (30 or higher of ACT | 92 or higher of the CLT).

Application Deadline: October 15

Application link:
https://www.lipscomb.edu/admissions/freshmen-admissions/types-aid/scholarships/trustee-scholarship

9 Carson-Newman University

Location: Jefferson City, Tennessee
Setting: Rural (90 Acres)
Undergraduate Enrollment: 1,695
Type: Private

F. Edward Hebert Armed Forces Health Professions Scholarship Program (HPSP): Full tuition for all four(4) years, plus a monthly stipend of $2,000 and a sign-on bonus of $20,000 in some cases.

Requirements: For health related majors | Contact admissions office for other requirements.

Application Deadline: Contact Admission Office.

Application link:
https://www.cn.edu/admissions-and-aid/financial-aid/types-of-aid/scholarships/

1 Texas Christian University

Location: Fort Worth, Texas
Setting: Suburban (302 Acres)
Undergraduate Enrollment: 10,222
Type: Private

Chancellor's Schoalrship: Awards 100% tuition & fees for all four (4) years.

Requirements: Top of admission pool academically.

Application Deadline: November 1

Application link: https://admissions.tcu.edu/afford/scholarship-aid/index.php

2 Abilene Christian University

Location: Abilene, Texas
Setting: City (272 Acres)
Undergraduate Enrollment: 3,560
Type: Private

National Merit Finalist & Semi-Finalists Schoalrship Award: Full tuition and fees for all four (4) years.

Requirements: Scholar must be a National Merit Finalist or semi-finalist. And must submit a FAFSA.

Application Deadline: November 1

Application link: https://acu.edu/admissions-aid/scholarships/first-year/

3   Trinity University

Location: San Antonio, Texas
Setting: Urban (125 Acres)
Undergraduate Enrollment: 2,526
Type: Private

Trinity Tower Scholarship: This scholarship awards covers full tuition over four (4) years.

Requirements: Excellent Academic and extracurricular record.

Application Deadline: November 1

Semmes Distingusied Scholars Scholarship: This scholarship awards covers full tuition over four (4) years. And a $5,000 stipend for research, travel and supplies.

Requirements: Strong Academic and extracurricular record. Applicant must be studying a STEM field at Trinity.

Application Deadline: November 1

Murchison Scholarship: This scholarship awards covers full tuition over four (4) years.

Requirements: Student should a high academic and extracurricular record.

Application Deadline: February 1

Application link:
https://www.trinity.edu/admissions-aid/tuition-and-financial-aid-admissions-and-aid

4   University of Houston

Location: Houston, Texas
Setting: Urban (895 Acres)
Undergraduate Enrollment: 38,581
Type: Public

National Merit Scholarship: This awards covers 100% tuition and fees for all four (4) years. Additionally, recipients receive a one-time $1,000 research stipend and a one-time $2,000 study abroad stipend.

Requirements: Applicants must be at the top of admission pool academically.

Army Reserve Officers' Training Corps (AROTC) Scholarship: Award takes care of full tuition for all four (4) years. Funds for books, equipment and supplies may also be provided.

Requirements: Contact Admission Office.

Application Deadline: Contact Admission Office.

Application link:
https://uh.edu/financial/undergraduate/types-aid/scholarships/

5 Lamar University

Location: Beaumont, Texas

Setting: Urban (292 Acres)

Undergraduate Enrollment: 8,394

Type: Public

Smith-Hutson Scholarship Program: This scholarship award covers 95% - 100% of recipient's college bill for all four (4) years.

Requirements: Applicant must be an entering freshaman to LU | Texas Resident | Submit FAFSA |

Application Deadline: February 1

Application link: https://www.lamar.edu/financial-aid/scholarships/smith-hutson-scholarship.html

6 Howard Payne University

Location: Brownwood, Texas

Setting: Rural (80 Acres)

Undergraduate Enrollment: 844

Type: Private

Gen. MacArthur Honors Scholarship: This scholarship program awards Full tuition for all four (4) years.

Requirements: Top 10% at an Accredited High School or 3.80 GPA) and (ACT 29 or SAT 1350 or CLT 91).

Application Deadline: Contact Admission Office.

Application link: https://www.hputx.edu/campus-offices/financial-aid/scholarships/

7 # Lubbock Christian University

Location: Lubbock, Texas
Setting: CIty (155 Acres)
Undergraduate Enrollment: 1,393
Type: Private

National Merit Scholarship: This awards covers Full tution for its recipients across 4-5 years.

Requirements: Student should be a National Merit Scholar to receive award.

Application Deadline: Contact Admission Office.

Application link: https://lcu.edu/financial-assistance/scholarships

8 # University of North Texas

Location: Denton, Texas
Setting: City (963 Acres)
Undergraduate Enrollment: 32,603
Type: Public

President's Elite Scholarship: This prestigious award covers full tuition for all four (4) years.

Requirements: High academic performance and good participation in extracurriccular activities.

Application Deadline: March 15

Application link: https://financialaid.unt.edu/unt-excellence-scholarships

Brigham Young University -- Provo

1

Location: Provo, Utah
Setting: City (560 Acres)
Undergraduate Enrollment: 31,633
Type: Private

The Russell M. Nelson Scholarship: This scholarship award covers full tuition, fees and more.

Requirements: Strong academic performance, extracurricular record, character and leadership history.

Application Deadline: Contact Admission Office.

National Merit Scholarship: Awards Full LDS tuition for eight semesters.

Check site for more details.

Eligibility: National Merit Finalist.

Heritage Scholarship: Awards Full LDS tuition for eight semesters.

Sterling Scholarship Competition: Awards Full LDS tuition for two semesters.

Check site for more details.

Application Deadline: December 15

Application link: https://enrollment.byu.edu/scholarship-types

2 Weber State University

Location: Ogden, Utah
Setting: Suburban (470 Acres)
Undergraduate Enrollment: 28,788
Type: Public

Presidential Scholarship: Scholarships covers full in-state tuition for four (4) years and $1,000 housing discount per year.

Requirements: Student should have a GPA of at least 3.2 and a SAT score of 1330 (29 ACT)

Application Deadline: December 1

Application link:
https://www.weber.edu/FinancialAid/resident.html

3 Southern Utah University

Location: Cedar City, Utah
Setting: Rural (129 Acres)
Undergraduate Enrollment: 12,080
Type: Public

President's Eight Semester Scholarship (For In-state students): Full tuition for all four (4) years.

Requirements: 3.9+ GPA 1390 – 1600 SAT Score, OR 31 – 36 ACT score.

President's Eight Semester Scholarship(For Out-of-State Students): Full tuition for all four (4) years.

Requirements: 3.9+ GPA 1390 – 1600 SAT Score, OR 31 – 36 ACT score.

Application Deadline: December 1

Application link:
https://www.suu.edu/finaid/scholarships.html

4 University of Utah

Location: Salt Lake City, Utah
Setting: Urban (1,534 Acres)
Undergraduate Enrollment: 25,826
Type: Public

For Utah Scholarship: 100% tuition and fees for all four (4) years.

Requirements: Utah residents who are eligible for PELL GRANT.

Application Deadline: February 1

President's Scholarship for Residents: Scholarships covers full in-state tuition for four (4) years .

Requirements: Based on cumulative GPA at admission, Course rigor considered.

Application Deadline: December 1

Application link:
https://financialaid.utah.edu/types-of-aid/scholarships/freshman/index.php

5 Utah State University

Location: Logan & Other Areas, Utah
Setting: City (450 Acres)
Undergraduate Enrollment: 24,255
Type: Public

Presidential Scholarship: Full tuition & fees for all four (4) years.

Requirements: Student should have at least a 3.75+ GPA and 1450+ SAT (OR 33 ACT).

Ambassador Scholarship: Full tuition & fees for all four (4) years.

Requirements: Must apply as a Senior in high school and have a GPA of 3.5 and above. (ACT/SAT not required)

Application Deadline: January 10

Application link:
https://www.usu.edu/admissions/costs-and-aid/#scholarships

6 Utah Tech University

Location: Saint George, Utah
Setting: City (117 Acres)
Undergraduate Enrollment: 12,201
Type: Public

Non-resident Presidential Scholarship: This award covers the whole tuition and fees for all four(4) years.

Requirements: Applicants are expected to have a GPA of atleast 3.2 and SAT score of 1300 (OR 28 ACT)

Resident Presidential Scholarship: This award covers the whole tuition and fees for all four(4) years.

Requirements: Applicants are expected to have a GPA of atleast 3.2 and SAT score of 1300 (OR 28 ACT)

Application Deadline: December 15 & July 15

Application link:
https://scholarships.utahtech.edu/non-resident-freshman-scholarships-2/

7 Utah Valley University

Location: Orem, Utah
Setting: City (524 Acres)
Undergraduate Enrollment: 40,542
Type: Public

Non-resident Presidential Scholarship: Full tuition & general fees for all four(4) years.

Requirements: Student should have atleast 3.9+ GPA and 1400+ SAT (OR 31 ACT).

Resident Presidential Scholarship: Full tuition & general fees for all four(4) years.

Requirements: Student should have atleast 3.9+ GPA and 1400+ SAT (OR 31 ACT).

Application Deadline: March 3

Application link:
https://www.uvu.edu/financialaid/scholarships/

1 Castleton University

Location: Castleton, Vermont
Setting: Rural (165 Acres)
Undergraduate Enrollment: 1,744
Type: Public

Valedictorian Scholarship: Full tuition for all four (4) years.

Requirements: Scholar must be a veledictorian with proof of this.

Application Deadline: Contact Admission Office.

Application link:
https://www.castleton.edu/admissions/scholarships-financial-aid/types-of-aid/scholarships/scholarships-for-first-year-applicants/

2 Norwich University

Location: Northfield, Vermont
Setting: Rural (1,200 Acres)
Undergraduate Enrollment: 2,988
Type: Private

Naval ROTC Preparatory Scholarship: Full tuition and fees for all four (4) plus years plus additional benefits.

Requirements: Visit scholarship page for detailed information.

Application Deadline: February 1

Application link:
https://www.norwich.edu/rotc/naval

3 ## University of Vermont

Location: Burlington, Vermont
Setting: Suburban (460 Acres)
Undergraduate Enrollment: 11,626
Type: Public

Green and Gold Scholars Award:
Scholarships covers full in-state tuition for all four years.

Requirements: Student must be nominated by a Vermont high and have high academic/extracurriclar track record.

Application Deadline: January 15

Application link:
https://www.uvm.edu/studentfinancialservices/scholarships_prospective_vermont_resident_students

4 ## Northern Vermont University

Location: Johnson and Lyndon, Vermont
Setting: Rural (350 Acres)
Undergraduate Enrollment: 1,706
Type: Public

Vermont Valedictorian Scholarship: Full tuition for all four (4) years.

Requirements: Vermonters who rank first in their high school classes.

Vermont Salutatorian Scholarship: Full tuition for all four (4) years.

Requirements: Vermonters who rank first in their high school classes.

Application Deadline: Contact Admission Office.

Application link:
https://www.northernvermont.edu/admissions-and-aid/financial-aid/nvu-scholarships/first-year-scholarships-for-vermonters/

1   Washington and Lee University

Location: Lexington, Virginia
Setting: City (430 Acres)
Undergraduate Enrollment: 1,857
Type: Private

Multiple Scholarship Awards: Full Tuition.

Requirements: Student should have excellent academic record and be from one of the following places: Maryland | West Virginia | New Orleans, Louisiana | Houston, Texas | Dallas, Texas | Columbia, South Carolina.

A full tuition scholarship is also available for students of Jewish faith specifically.

Fully funded need based scholarships are also available.

Application Deadline: Visit Scholarship Page.

Application link:
https://www.wlu.edu/admissions/scholarships-and-aid/types-of-aid/scholarships/additional-scholarships/

2   Christendom College

Location: Front Royal, Virginia
Setting: Suburban (200 Acres)
Undergraduate Enrollment: 539
Type: Private

Padre Pio Full-Tuition Scholarship: Full tuition

Requirements: SAT 1280+ OR ACT 27+ OR CLT 84+ and an admission to Christendom College.

Application link:
https://www.christendom.edu/admissions/full-tuition-scholarship/

Military Service Scholarship Program: Full Tuition.

Requirements: For more information on how to apply and program eligibility, please contact Christine Schmidt, Financial Aid Officer, at christine.schmidt@christendom.edu or **540-551-9216**.

Application Deadline: Contact admission office.

Application link:
https://www.christendom.edu/admissions/financial-aid/military-service-scholarship-program/

3 Liberty University

Location: Lynchburg, Virginia
Setting: City (7,000 Acres)
Undergraduate Enrollment: 48,135
Type: Private

Liberty Academic Scholarship:
Awards Full tuition.

Requirements: Test score; SAT 1540+ OR ACT 35+ OR CLT 107+ combined with a High school GPA of 3.0+

Application Deadline: Contact Admission Office.

Application link:
https://www.liberty.edu/student-financial-services/scholarships/

4 Saint Michael's College

Location: Colchester, Virginia
Setting: Suburban (440 Acres)
Undergraduate Enrollment: 1,421
Type: Private

Presidential Scholarship: Awards range from $17,000 up to Full tuition for all four(4) plus years.

Requirements: Student must be nominated by a Vermont high school and meet the following requirements: A- average or higher, Top 10% of class, 1300+ SAT or 27+ ACT test score(test-optional)

Application Deadline: November 1

Application link:
https://www.smcvt.edu/admission-aid/financial-aid/scholarships-loans-grants-and-work-study/academic-scholarships/

5 Hollins University

Location: Roanoke, Virginia
Setting: Suburban (475 Acres)
Undergraduate Enrollment: 713
Type: Private

Batten Scholar Award: Awards 100% tuition for all four (4) years.

Requirements: Top of admission pool academically.

Application Deadline: December 1

Application link:
https://hollins.edu/admission/undergraduate-financial-aid-scholarships/scholarships-awards/

6 Bridgewater College

Location: Bridgewater, Virginia
Setting: Rural (300 Acres)
Undergraduate Enrollment: 1,427
Type: Private

President's Merit Award: Full tuition for all four (4) years.

Requirements: Strong academic record.

Application Deadline: January 28

Application link:
https://www.bridgewater.edu/admissions-aid/tuition-and-financial-aid/financial-aid/

7 Hampden-Sydney College

Location: Hampden-Sydney, Virginia
Setting: Rural (1,343 Acres)
Undergraduate Enrollment: 851
Type: Private

The Davis Fellowship: Award covers full tuition.

Requirements: Strong Academic and extracurricular record.

Application Deadline: Contact Admission Office -- Telephone: (800) 755-0733
Email: hsfinaid@hsc.edu

Application link:
https://www.hsc.edu/admission-and-financial-aid/financial-aid/types-of-aid/academic-and-leadership-awards

8 Virginia Wesleyan University

Location: Virginia Beach, Virginia
Setting: Suburban (300 Acres)
Undergraduate Enrollment: 1,241
Type: Private

The Batten Fellowship: Awards 100% tuition for all four (4) years.

Requirements: High academic performance specifically 1353+ in SAT (or equivalent), 3.5+ high school GPA, and application to Batten Honors College.

Application Deadline: March 9

Application link:
https://www.vwu.edu/enrollment-aid/financial-aid/vwu-grants-and-scholarships.php

9 Bluefield University

Location: Bluefield, Virginia
Setting: Rural (82 Acres)
Undergraduate Enrollment: 753
Type: Private

Presidential Scholarship: Award covers full tuition for all four (4) years.

Requirements: Good academic and extracurriccular record

Application Deadline: Contact Admission Office.

Application link:
https://www.bluefield.edu/bluefield-central/financial-aid/grants-scholarships/

10 University of Virginia

Location: Charlottesville, Virginia
Setting: Suburban (1,682 Acres)
Undergraduate Enrollment: 17,299
Type: Public

Reserved Officers' Training Corps Scholarships: Awards 100% tuition and fees for all four (4) years — recipient could also receive monthly stipends, books allowance and supplies.

Requirements: Varies across Army, Navy & Airforce — Visit scholarship page.

Application Deadline: Visit web page.

Application link:
https://sfs.virginia.edu/financial-aid-new-applicants/financial-aid-basics/types-aid/scholarships-and-grants

11 Virginia Commonwealth University

Location: Richmond, Virginia
Setting: Urban (198 Acres)
Undergraduate Enrollment: 21,394
Type: Public

Provost Scholarship: Full tuition and mandatory fees.

Requirements: A minimum 4.0 GPA and 1200+ in SAT (and it's equivalent in other tests)

Application Deadline: November 1

Application link:
https://admissions.vcu.edu/cost-aid/scholarships-funding/

1 Seattle Pacific University

Location: Seattle, Washington
Setting: Urban (44 Acres)
Undergraduate Enrollment: 2,640
Type: Private

Distinguished Scholar Award: Award covers Full tuition.

Requirements: Good academic and extracurricular record (Invitatation only)

Application link: https://spu.edu/undergraduate-admissions/scholarships-financial-aid/scholarships-and-grants/first-year-student-scholarships

Falcon Bound Scholarship: Full tuition

Requirements: 1220/25 or higher in SAT/ACT, 3.0 high school GPA, eligible for College Bound, etc.

Application Deadline: December 15

Application link: https://spu.edu/student-financial-services/grants-and-scholarships/scholarships/falcon-bound

2 Pacific Lutheran University

Location: Tacoma, Washington
Setting: Suburban (156 Acres)
Undergraduate Enrollment: 2,373
Type: Private

Regent's Scholarship: Awards covers Full tuition.

Requirements: High school seniors who have demonstrated significant leadership and service, and have achieved a cumulative GPA of 3.8 (weighted), or scored 1310 or higher on the SAT (math and evidence-based reading and writing only), or scored 28 or higher on the ACT.

Application Deadline: December 1

Application link: https://www.plu.edu/student-financial-services/types-of-aid/scholarships-and-grants/

3 Walla Walla University

Location: College Place, Washington
Setting: Rural (83 Acres)
Undergraduate Enrollment: 1,419
Type: Private

National Merit Finalists Awards: 100% tuition for two years and 50% tuition for two additional years.

Requirements: Finalist in the national merit competition.

Application Deadline: Contact Admission Counselor

Application link:
https://www.wallawalla.edu/admissions/student-financial-services/financial-aid/scholarships/freshman-scholarships-2022-23/

4 Whitworth University

Location: Spokane, Washington
Setting: Suburban (200 Acres)
Undergraduate Enrollment: 2,307
Type: Private

Whitworth Bound Promise: Awards up to Full tuition.

Requirements: Offered and renewed to Washington residents who are eligible for the College Bound Scholarship and have a minimum 3.0 weighted, cumulative GPA.

Application Deadline: Contact Admission Office.

Application link:
https://www.whitworth.edu/cms/administration/financial-aid/whitworth-scholarships-for-first-year-students/

5 Washington State University -- Pullman

Location: Pullman, Washington
Setting: Rural (1,742 Acres)
Undergraduate Enrollment: 24,278
Type: Public

Distinguished Regents Scholars: Full tuition and mandatory fees.

Requirements: Strong academic achievement, co-curricular/civic involvement, academic reference.

Application Deadline: Contact sfs.regentsscholars@wsu.edu or 509-335-9711

National Merit Scholarship: Awards up to Full tuition.

Requirements: National Merit Scholarship and WSU – Pullman admission.

Application Deadline: Admission by Jan 31 and choose WSU as first choice on National Merit Corporation by May 1

Application link: https://admission.wsu.edu/scholarships/scholarship-awards/regents/

6 Whitman College

Location: Walla Walla, Washington
Setting: Rural (117 Acres)
Undergraduate Enrollment: 1,559
Type: Private

The Eells Scholarship: Awards Full tuition and fees.

Requirements: Entering student who has financial need and demonstrates high academic achievement and talent in fine/performing arts or humanities.

Application Deadline: January 15

Application link: https://www.whitman.edu/admission-and-aid/financial-aid-and-costs/merit-and-talent-awards

1 Bethany College

Location: Bethany, West Virginia
Setting: Rural (1,100 Acres)
Undergraduate Enrollment: 569
Type: Private

Presidential Scholarship: Awards Full tuition.

Requirements: Contact Admission for more info: 304-829-7611

Application Deadline: Contact Admission for more info: 304-829-7611

Application link:
https://www.bethanywv.edu/admissions-aid/affording-bethany-college/scholarships/

2 Bluefield State College

Location: Bluefield, West Virginia
Setting: Rural (50 Acres)
Undergraduate Enrollment: 1,358
Type: Public

BOG Auxiliary Scholarship: Full tuition and/or fees.

Requirements: Academic Excellence as determined by ACT/SAT score and GPA.

Application Deadline: Contact admission office.

Application link:
https://bluefieldstate.edu/tuition/scholarships

Marquette University

Location: Milwaukee, Wisconsin
Setting: Urban (107 Acres)
Undergraduate Enrollment: 7,660
Type: Private

Urban Scholars Program: Awards Full tuition plus housing.

Requirements: 3.0/4.0 GPA, Demostrated leadership and service, Demonstrated financial need (FAFSA or Net price calculator), High school seniors from Milwaukee area.

P.S: Citizenship is not a factor in awarding scholarship.

Application Deadline: February 1

Ronald E. And Kathleen M. Zupko Scholarship: Awards Full tuition.

Requirements: High School Seniors in the Milwaukee Public School System (with 3.0 GPA or higher), Demonstrated financial need (FAFSA or Net Price Calculator)

Application Deadline: February 1

Burke Scholars Program: Awards Full tuition.

Requirements: Wisconsin high school seniors or entering first-year students, demonstrated community service, demonstrated academic excellence through high GPA, SAT/ACT and application materials.

Opus Scholars Program: Awards Full tuition, plus student fees and lab fees | conditionally housing and meal plans are also awarded.

Requirements: Admission to Opus College of Engineering, community service (e.g. Cristo Rey Network), demonstrated financial need (FAFSA or Net Price Calculator)

Do Great Things Full Tuition Scholarship: Awards Full tuition plus 2 years of room and board.

Requirements: Admission to Marquette University, attended Green Bay West High School, demonstrated financial need (FAFSA or Net Price Calculator)

Global Scholar Scholarship Award: Full tuition.

Requirements: Freshman entering Marquette University, high school located outside United States, 3.25 GPA (on an unweighted 4.0 scale), international student on an F-1 visa.

Application Deadline: December 1

Application link: https://www.marquette.edu/explore/scholarships.php

2 Carroll University

Location: Waukesha, Wisconsin
Setting: Suburban (137 Acres)
Undergraduate Enrollment: 2,884
Type: Private

MacAllister Scholarship: Awards Full tuition.

Requirements: Applicants must be accepted to Carroll University, good academic performance and extracurricular activities.

Application Deadline: December 2

Application link:
https://www.carrollu.edu/financial-aid/undergraduate-scholarships/macallister

3 University of Wisconsin, Platteville

Location: Plattevile, Wisconsin
Setting: Rural (820 Acres)
Undergraduate Enrollment: 6,266
Type: Public

Pioneer Plegde Award: Awards Full tuition and fees.

Requirements: Be a freshman (full time), submit FAFSA and be Pell eligible, be resident of Wisconsin, Illinois, Iowa or Minnesota.

Application Deadline: May 1

Application link:
https://www.uwplatt.edu/types-scholarships#freshman-scholarships

4

University of Wisconsin – River Falls

Location: River Falls, Wisconsin
Setting: Suburban (303 Acres)
Undergraduate Enrollment: 5,003
Type: Public

Chancellor Scholars Scholarship: Full tuition or Half Tuition + $2,000.

Requirements: Must have a high school GPA of 3.8 or higher **OR** rank in the top 10% of their high school class **OR** have an 28 ACT (1310 SAT) or higher.

- Applicant Must submit one letter of recommendation from a teacher, guidance counselor, coach, mentor, etc. explaining the student's leadership and academic potential.

- Applicant Must write an essay.

Application Deadline: January 5

Mary Barrett Chancellor Scholars Scholarship: Full tuition or Half Tuition + $2,000.

Requirements: Must have a minimum ACT score of 26 and/or a high school GPA of 3.0

This application includes an essay and digital portfolio upload requirement. Finalists will be required to complete an interview and provide a physical portfolio containing work samples.

The award is for four academic years, provided the student continues to pursue a degree in Art: BS Art, BS Art Education, BFA

Application Deadline: February 1

Application link: https://www.uwrf.edu/paying-for-college/scholarships

5 Viterbo University

Location: La Crosse, Wisconsin
Setting: City (21 Acres)
Undergraduate Enrollment: 1,660
Type: Private

Health Science Scholarship: Awards Full tuition (For Health related Majors only)

Requirements: Great academic performance, and strong extracurricular activities, reference from science teacher or school counselor.

Application Deadline: January 15

Application link:
https://www.viterbo.edu/school-natural-science-mathematics-and-engineering/scholarship-opportunities

6 Milwaukee School of Engineering

Location: Milwaukee, Wisconsin
Setting: Urban (22 Acres)
Undergraduate Enrollment: 2,510
Type: Private

ROTC Programs & Scholarships: Awards range from $18,000 up to Full tuition and fees.

Requirements: Visit scholarship page for more details

Application Deadline: Visit scholarship page for more details

Application link:
https://www.msoe.edu/admissions-aid/financial-aid-scholarships/scholarships-and-grants/rotc-scholarships/navy-rotc/

7 Ripon College

Location: Ripon, Wisconsin
Setting: City (250 Acres)
Undergraduate Enrollment: 810
Type: Private

Knop Science Scholarship: Awards Full tuition.

Requirements: Academic and extracurricular excellence. This scholarship application process is by invitation only. It is open to majors in science and mathematics departments.

Application Deadline: February 1

Application link: https://ripon.edu/financial-aid/scholarships/

8 University of Wisconsin, Oshkosh

Location: Oshkosh, Wisconsin
Setting: City (166 Acres)
Undergraduate Enrollment: 14,068
Type: Public

Army ROTC Scholarship: Full in-state tuition, books and cash stipends.

Requirements: Visit scholarship page for more information.

Application Deadline: June 20

Application link: https://uwosh.edu/admissions/costs-and-aid/scholarships/

9 Alverno College

Location: Milwaukee, Wisconsin
Setting: Urban (47 Acres)
Undergraduate Enrollment: 1,099
Type: Private

Roosevelt Scholarship: Awards Full tuition.

Requirements: Good academic performance and excellence in leadership/volunteerism.

Application Deadline: December 2

Application link: https://www.alverno.edu/Financial-Aid-Scholarships

10

Carthage College

Location: Kenosha, Wisconsin
Setting: Suburban (80 Acres)
Undergraduate Enrollment: 2,637
Type: Private

Presidential Scholarship: $27,000 to Full tuition.

Requirements: Excellent academic performance & extracurricular activities, 250-word essay, submitted Carthage college application, presidential scholarship competition application.

Business Scholarships: Full tuition (for business related majors)

Requirements: Carthage college application, one-page essay, business scholarship competition application, excellent grades, test scores and extracurricular activities.

Kenosha Scholarships: Full tuition (for Kenosha residents only)

Requirements: Carthage college application, 250-word essay, Kenosha scholarship competition application, excellent grades, test scores and extracurricular activities.

Math/Science Scholarships: Full tuition (for Science and math related majors)

Requirements: Carthage college application, one-page essay, math/science scholarship competition application, excellent grades, test scores and extracurricular activities.

Spring Scholarships: Full tuition (for Science and math related majors)

Requirements: Carthage college admission, spring scholarship competition application, excellent grades, test scores and extracurricular activities.

Application Deadline: November

Kenosha Police/Fire Scholarship: Full tuition (for Science and math related majors)

Requirements: Dependent of a city of Kenosha Police officer or firefighter, Carthage college application, scholarship application, good grades, test scores and extracurricular activities.

Application Deadline: December 3

Application link: https://www.carthage.edu/admissions/undergraduate-students/undergraduate-scholarships/

Wyoming Catholic College

Location: Lander, Wyoming
Setting: Town (600 Acres)
Undergraduate Enrollment: 189
Type: Private

Founder's Scholarship: Awards Full tuition.

Requirements: High school senior(s) who applied to Wyoming Catholic College. Students who exhibit academic excellence throughout the application eassy, letters of reference, and high school (unofficial) transcript.

Application Deadline: October 1 (for Fall) & February 1 (for spring)

Application link: https://wyomingcatholic.edu/admissions/scholarships/

CHAPTER (2)

SCHOLARSHIP APPLICATION TIPS

Dear scholarship award aspirants, we have listed out the various full tuition scholarships that are available for undergraduate study at universities and colleges in the United States. These scholarships are available to both U.S. residents and international students (unless otherwise indicated).

Instead of writing wordy sentences, we will go straight to giving the key scholarship tips!

With the aid of this book, aspirants can have a full view of suitable universities/colleges they can apply to and gain financial aid.

Here are Key Guidelines/Tips to Aid Students Win Scholarships

➤ **Apply By Early Action**: Students are advised to apply early in order to be duly considered for scholarship awards. The scholarship application for some schools goes together with the application for admissions, while other scholarship programs require entirely separate applications for them. Be sure to apply well ahead of the scholarship deadline(s).
Note: Confirm the deadline of the scholarship and make sure you beat the deadline. Applications submitted after deadlines are usually disregarded.

➤ **Fill & Submit FAFSA**: Fill out and submit your FAFSA before the deadline. Filing a FAFSA is a requirement for many full ride scholarships. You'll learn more on the key definitions page of this book.

➤ **Apply For Scholarships You are Most Qualified For:** Scholarships have their requirements, these are put in place to provide the awards to deserving students. Therefore, it is highly advisable that you apply only for scholarships that you meet their requirements. It is also worth noting that meeting the minimum requirements doesn't guarantee that you'll obtain the scholarship. Why? Scholarships are competitive you should present yourself in the best way possible – by exuding excellence – to stand a chance. Scholarship opportunities at less known/less populated schools have shown to be easier to get.

➤ **Have a Good Test Score & GPA | Unique Talent:** SATs, ACTs, CLTs, and other grading system test scores should have been taken and scores obtained before applying for scholarships. A high test score combined with a superb high school GPA will increase the chances of you getting a scholarship as the majority of full ride scholarships are centered around the academic performance of scholars. Other criteria like leadership abilities, cultural background, unique talent, or life challenges are considered for some scholarships.

➢ **Craft Your Applications/ Essays to Impress:** Pay close attention to application essay topics and do thorough work in crafting a well-written essay and write to impress the reviewer highlighting your achievements in a very impressive manner. Ensure that your essay is well structured and free of any errors. Write award-winning essays!

➢ **Apply for as Many Scholarships as Possible:** Do not limit yourself to one scholarship. In as much as you meet the requirements for scholarships, give it your best shot. Several students have received multiple full ride scholarship offers from which they chose the best – that can be your story too.

➢ **Get Outstanding Recommendations/Nominations**: For scholarships requiring Nominations please ensure that you're nominated on time. Also, ensure that your recommendation letters show how much of an outstanding student you are.

➢ **Prepare Properly for Scholarship Interviews:** If the scholarship you apply for requires you to go through an interview process, prepare properly for it. Take your interview session with confidence.

➢ **DO NOT FALL Victim for Scholarship Scams.** Apply directly to the University/College of your interest or on the *official website* of the external scholarship(s) you wish to apply for. Do not enrich fraudsters using unauthorized means in applying for scholarships.

A Typical Scholarship Award Process

Find Scholarship(s) ➡ Start Application ➡ Submit Documents ➡

Submit Application ➡ Attend Interview (*Not applicable in all cases*)

⬇

$ *Receive Scholarship/Get Feedback*

✉ **Contact Us Here: https://bit.ly/chrisnuel-publishing**

Definition of Key Terms

What is FAFSA?

FAFSA stands for Free Application for Federal Student Aid.

To apply for federal student aid, such as federal grants, work-study, and loans, you need to complete the Free Application for Federal Student Aid (**FAFSA**®).

Some scholarship awards listed in this book require you to complete a FAFSA and to file it every year in order to get a renewal. Completing the FAFSA is not so much of a hassle – it is quite straightforward.

You can learn more about the FAFSA here; https://studentaid.gov/help/fafsa

A recommended FAFSA resource is "FAFSA Guru" on YouTube.

Who is a National Merit Scholar?

Started in 1955, the National Merit Scholarship Program is an academic scholarship competition for recognition and university scholarships, which is administered and managed by the National Merit Scholarship Corporation (NMSC). The NMSC is a privately funded, not-for-profit organization based in Evanston, Illinois.

Approximately 1.5 million high school students enter the program each year. Students are required to take the PSAT/NMSQT® and undergo some other evaluation process to be chosen as finalists.

Students who are chosen as semifinalists and finalist(s) may be eligible for some financial awards and recognitions.

The goal, however, should be for students to be selected as finalists (National Merit Scholars). National merit scholars receive special recognition and have access to National Merit® $2500 Scholarships, Corporate-sponsored Merit Scholarship awards, and College-sponsored Merit Scholarship awards.

College-sponsored scholarships in most cases can be up to full-ride or full-tuition scholarships.

Definition of Key Terms

What is PSAT/NMSQT?

The PSAT/NMSQT stands for Preliminary SAT/National Merit Scholarship Qualifying Test. PSAT/NMSQT is a standardized test administered by the College Board and co-sponsored by the National Merit Scholarship Corporation (NMSC). It is taken by millions of students each year.

The test scores from the PSAT/NMSQT are used to selected National Merit Scholars.

What are Test Scores?

Standardized tests are administered in the US each year for college admissions and other academic related activities. The college standardized tests in the US are:

- SAT

- ACT

- CLT (Accepted by a few schools)

High scores on these standardized tests (coupled with a high GPA) will give students a better chance of securing a full ride scholarship.

What to Expect in Future Editions of "The Full Tuition Scholarship Book"

?

In summary, you should expect more amazing scholarship opportunities.

Future editions of this book will be updated with the latest full tuition scholarships available in the United States – from institutional to external/private, and even to the most hidden.

✉ **Contact Us Here: https://bit.ly/chrisnuel-publishing1**

Other Scholarship Titles

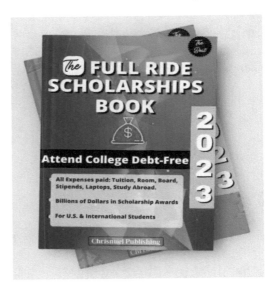

The Full Ride Scholarships Book: Attend College Debt-Free

⌘ Link to Book:

https://www.amazon.com/Full-Ride-Scholarships-Book-2023/dp/B0BD7PMKZC

ENJOY YOUR SCHOLARSHIPS !!!

Notes

Notes

11955204R10124